Predestination

THE COMBINED EDITION OF

Biblical Predestination

AND

Predestination
in the Old Testament

Gordon H. Clark

Presbyterian and Reformed Publishing Company
Phillipsburg, New Jersey

Originally published in two separate volumes:

Biblical Predestination
Copyright 1969
Presbyterian and Reformed Publishing Company

Predestination in the Old Testament
Copyright 1978
Presbyterian and Reformed Publishing Company

Combined edition
Copyright 1987
Lois A. Zeller and Elizabeth Clark George

Manufactured in the United States of America

Library of Congress Cataloging-in-Publication Data

Clark, Gordon Haddon.
  Predestination: the combined edition of Biblical
predestination and Predestination in the Old Testament.

  Includes index.
  1. Predestination—Biblical teaching. I. Clark,
Gordon Haddon, Predestination in the Old Testament.
1987. II. Title.
BS680.P65C57   1987   234'.9   87-16815
ISBN 0-87552-169-X

CONTENTS

PART ONE: BIBLICAL PREDESTINATION   1

Introduction   1

1. Creation   7

2. Omniscience   31

3. The Eternal Decree and Its Execution   47

4. Pre-destination   66

5. Regeneration   85

6. Free Will   110

7. Epilogue   145

PART TWO: PREDESTINATION IN THE OLD TESTAMENT   151

Index of Scripture   207

Books by Gordon H. Clark:

Readings in Ethics (1931)
Selections from Hellenistic Philosophy (1940)
A History of Philosophy (1941)
A Christian Philosophy of Education (1946)
A Christian View of Men and Things (1952)
What Presbyterians Believe (1956)
Thales to Dewey (1957)
Dewey (1960)
Religion, Reason, and Revelation (1961, 1986)
William James (1963)
Karl Barth's Theological Method (1963)
The Philosophy of Science and Belief in God (1964)
What Do Presbyterians Believe? (1965, 1985)
Peter Speaks Today (1967)
The Philosophy of Gordon H. Clark (1968)
Biblical Predestination (1969)
Historiography: Secular and Religious (1971)
II Peter (1972)
The Johannine Logos (1972)
Three Types of Religious Philosophy (1973)
First Corinthians (1975)
Predestination in the Old Testament (1978)
Colossians (1979)
I and II Peter (1980)
Language and Theology (1980)
First John (1980)
God's Hammer (1982)
Behaviorism and Christianity (1982)
Faith and Saving Faith (1983)
In Defense of Theology (1984)
The Pastoral Epistles (1984)
The Biblical Doctrine of Man (1984)
The Trinity (1985)
Logic (1985)
Ephesians (1985)
Clark Speaks From the Grave (1986)
Logical Criticisms of Textual Criticism (1986)
The Atonement (1986)
First and Second Thessalonians (1986)

Part One

BIBLICAL PREDESTINATION

INTRODUCTION

One evening I attended a large tent meeting in Indianápolis. In the middle of the sermon as the evangelist warmed up to his subject, he launched into an attack on predestination; or to make the situation clear, one might say that the evangelist attacked the Calvinistic doctrine of predestination. After about ten minutes of this, he seemed to be satisfied that he had pretty well made his point. But he hesitated a moment. Perhaps a fleeting thought occurred to him that after all the Bible does indeed speak of predestination. So he added, "Of course," and I particularly noted the *of course*, "I accept what the Bible teaches about predestination." The only trouble was that he never gave his audience the least hint of what he thought the Bible teaches.

If the Bible has something to say about predestination, surely we ought not to skip those passages. But many people would like to. They say the doctrine is controversial and should not be discussed. This is what a Bible teacher told his class in an allegedly Christian college. Predestination is controversial. One of the students was a young Bulgarian. He wanted to learn and to preach the gospel. He listened to the professor and dutifully took in his words. Not wishing to delay his Christian service, he took a Sunday School class of Bulgarian laborers in Chicago. Here he could teach them the simple Gospel. But to his amazement they questioned him on predestination. The poor young man— he had accepted his teacher's advice, had never studied the subject, and could not minister to his people.

1

It is strange too that this semi-Christian college, with its aversion to controversial doctrines, did not mind taking insistent positions on other doctrines that were equally controversial among Christians. Equally controversial and much less important. It would seem that those who decry controversy mean to prevent others from disputing their own peculiarities.

There are, however, more reputable, less superficial, more scholarly Christians who have issued warnings about studying this doctrine. One of these gentlemen was Calvin himself, whom the evangelist so disliked.

In the *Institutes*, Book III, xxi, 1-2, Calvin wrote, "The discussion of predestination—a subject of itself rather intricate—is made very perplexed, and therefore dangerous, by human curiosity, which no barriers can restrain from wandering into forbidden labyrinths, and soaring beyond its sphere, as if determined to leave none of the divine secrets unscrutinized or unexplored. As we see multitudes everywhere guilty of this arrogance and presumption . . . it is proper to admonish them of the bounds of their duty on this subject."

Calvin did not explain who these people were who tried to leave no divine secret unscrutinized. Undoubtedly there were such people in his day. But in the twentieth century the opposite trouble plagues the Christian community. There are too few people who wish to understand even the simplest biblical teaching. This is not a theological age. Some writers say that it is a post-Christian age. What is needed today is an exhortation to study the Bible. And it would seem that there is less danger in studying the Bible than in ignoring it.

Indeed in the next few lines Calvin says much the same thing. "It is unreasonable that man should scrutinize with impunity those things that the Lord has determined to be

2

hidden in himself; . . . The secret of his will which he determined to reveal to us, he discovers in his Word." It is not only *unreasonable* to scrutinize the hidden will of God, as Calvin says; it is impossible. Knowledge of predestination is to be sought in God's revealed will, in the Word, and in the Word alone. Let us not pry elsewhere with that curiosity that Calvin condemns, but let us not neglect to study carefully what God reveals to us and intends that we should study.

Calvin also has some words for those who would shut their eyes to God's revelation. "Others," he says, "desirous of remedying this evil [of presumption] will have all mention of predestination to be as it were buried; they teach men to avoid every question concerning it as they would a precipice. . . . Whatever therefore is declared in the Scripture concerning predestination, we must be cautious not to withhold from believers, lest we appear to defraud them of the favor of their God, or to reprove and censure the Holy Spirit for publishing what it would be useful by any means to suppress."

It is to be noted that Calvin was intent on reproving those who wished to speculate on some other basis than the Word of God. The following study will keep as close as possible to the Scripture. Examination of biblical texts will fill every page. The Bible was addressed to all classes of people. It was not intended to be read only by priests or scholars. The Epistle of Paul to the Romans, which is rightly regarded as somewhat difficult, was addressed to "all that be in Rome, beloved of God, called to be saints." Many of these people were slaves. No doubt the majority of the Christians in Rome came from the lower classes. They had not had a high school education. Some of them could neither read nor write. But Paul expected them, if not to read, at least to hear the reading of his letter. Anyone who warns Christians to stay away from any part of the Scripture

3

violates the address on Paul's letter and presumes to know better than God what Christians should learn.

A study of the Bible will show that predestination is not an obscure doctrine or one infrequently mentioned. It permeates the Bible and turns out to be very fundamental. Many places where the word itself is not used, the idea is present. This is one of the points to be made by the following careful examination of many passages. For example, this study will begin with the first verse of Genesis. It speaks of creation. Predestination is not mentioned. But the kind of creation described in this first verse and other verses that tell about God's act of creating could not have occurred without the divine predestinating forethought and intention.

Should we treat the subject carefully? Well, of course, we should. The Westminster Confession, which defines Presbyterian doctrine, says in chapter III, section viii, "The doctrine of this high mystery of predestination is to be handled with special prudence and care, that men attending the will of God revealed in his Word, and yielding obedience thereunto, may from the certainty of their effectual vocation, be assured of their eternal election. . . ." But to avoid the doctrine altogether is not to handle it with care. To avoid the doctrine is to undermine the Christian's assurance of salvation and to detract from the glory of God.

Handle it with care; but handle it by God's command. Some think they can add to the doctrine material from human experience and discover the secrets that God has not revealed; let us on the other hand not think that the Scripture is particularly limited and narrow. God has in fact revealed a great deal. We are not supposed to take each verse in isolation and restrict ourselves to disjointed bits of scattered information. We are to compare Scripture with Scripture. What is not clear or complete in one verse may be clearer or may be completed in another. We are to infer and deduce. If the Bible teaches that David was king of Israel and if it also teaches that Solomon was a son of David, we can legitimately infer that Solomon was the son of a king of Israel. No doubt we should avoid putting two and two together and getting five; but we do God no honor if we never get even three. The Westminster Confession, quoted just above, says in chapter I, section vi, "The whole counsel of God . . . is either expressly set down in Scripture, or by good and necessary consequence may be deduced from Scripture." Every minister does this when he preaches a sermon. Sermons are not just quotations of verses. The good pastor explains what the verse means, and in his explanation uses other passages that will help us to understand. Anything else would be foolish. It is foolish therefore when false teachers try to prevent us from examining the verses on predestination and putting two and two together to make four. What is universally done with other doctrines cannot be denied in this case.

Now, we do not want to add two and two and get five. But is not the greater danger that we shall only get three? God's infinite wisdom is far more than we can fathom. Not only is his secret will beyond our reach, but it is also unlikely that any one of us should see all that he has revealed for our understanding. God indeed said that *all* Scripture is profitable for doctrine; none of it is beyond understanding; but each of us misses a good part of it. Recall how Jesus rebuked his disciples on the road to Emmaus, "O slow of heart to believe all that the prophets have spoken . . . and beginning at Moses and all the prophets he expounded unto them in all the Scriptures the things concerning himself." Remember also that out of the title, God of Abraham, Jesus deduced the doctrine of the future life that the Sadducees denied. How many of us would have seen that lesson in that divine title? There must be innumerable truths in the Bible that escape our minds.

5

Our danger is not in finding too much, but in finding too little.

On the other hand, we should not set aside the study in the fear that everything will be impossibly difficult. God intended that we study the Bible. Some of his revelation is very deep. But there are also easy lessons, for Roman slaves, and those who have no high school education. If God has mailed us a letter, let us read it with care.

Chapter One

CREATION

As was said a few lines ago, a study of predestination can well begin with the doctrine of creation. The reason for this is that all of God's acts reflect his character or nature. A Mohammedan doctrine of predestination would differ from the Christian doctrine because Islam and Christianity have two different concepts of God. Now, the first act of God in time is his creation of the universe. Whether we wish to think of the creation of angels, or merely of the physical world and man, creation shows something about God. It tells us something very important about the kind of God with whom we have to do. Just what this important information is will come out more definitely as the study proceeds. Thus Genesis One will serve as a start.

1. GOD CREATED ALL THINGS

"In the beginning God created the heavens and the earth. . . . So God created man in his own image. . . . Thus the heavens and the earth were finished, and all the host of them." This last phrase comes from Genesis 2:1.

In these verses there are two things to be particularly noted. They are really in these verses, just as the future life is in the title, God of Abraham. But that these two things are really in these verses will be more clearly understood when they are compared with other parts of Scripture. By comparison and deduction, summaries are formed, and then we have doctrine. Now, the two things in these

7

early verses in Genesis are the notion of creation and its application to all things.

Since this second point, the "all things," is the easier to understand, we shall start with it. Genesis 1:1 says that God created the heavens and the earth. This is very inclusive. It almost covers all things. But not quite. It does not mention angels. Before we can say that God created absolutely everything, it will be necessary to find some indication that he created angels. This will have to wait. But the phrase, "the heavens and the earth . . . and all the host of them," can certainly be taken to cover all the physical universe. Genesis 1:27 mentions the creation of man. Genesis 2:7 gives a more detailed description of this creation: "The Lord God formed man of the dust of the ground, and breathed into his nostrils the breath of life and man became a living soul." This indicates that creation includes more than the physical universe. It includes the life that was given to the body that had been formed of dust. Life is something additional to dust, earth, clay. God is the source of man's life. These several items are a good part of the whole creation. They go a long way toward showing that God created absolutely everything.

If the items explicitly mentioned so far are not yet enough for the inference that God created absolutely everything, supporting passages, both by their added detail and by their greater generality, will leave no doubt remaining. Note carefully how much they take in.

Psalm 89:12. "The north and the south, thou hast created them." This is a bit of detail, but just a bit. One cannot be sure what north and south mean here. North may mean Tabor and Hermon, and south might mean Egypt. But it would also fit into the theme of the Psalm, with its references to the heavens, to suppose that north means the region of the north star. The verse obviously wants to indicate the great extent of God's creation, but perhaps the most we can get from this verse logically is that God created many things.

More information can be obtained from Psalm 104:30, "Thou sendest forth thy spirit, they are created." Verse 30 must be understood in the light of verse 24, "O Lord, how manifold are thy works." The creation in verse 30 takes in all the works of God. Specifically mentioned are the heavens, the clouds, angels, water, grass, cattle, trees, hills, birds, moon, sun, young lions, and creeping things innumerable: "Thou sendest forth thy spirit, they are created."

In one way this is reminiscent of Genesis 2:7. As God breathed into Adam's nostrils the breath or spirit of life, so too God sent forth his spirit into the animals. Some people are afraid to say that animals have souls. They not only have souls, they are souls. Some people are afraid to say that animals have spirit. But Genesis 6:17 and 7:15, and Psalm 104:29, as well as Ecclesiastes 3:21 ascribe spirit to animals. Animals are souls. They are not just clay. God created life as well as stones and mud. Of course, Psalm 104 mentions stones and mud, or at least, water and hills. But beyond these it mentions one thing that was missing in Genesis, namely, angels. If it was the existence of angels that prevented us from inferring that God created absolutely everything, that stumbling block is now removed.

Perhaps someone may say that verse four, where angels are mentioned, is too far way from verse 30 where creation is mentioned. It really is not: both verses are in the same Psalm and one theme runs throughout. But since even the best of scholars make mistakes, since the rest of us make many mistakes, and since we should handle the Word of God with care and caution, it is good policy to use many verses to establish a doctrine. No doctrine should be based on a single text.

On one occasion I objected to what a Bible teacher was saying. I thought he was mistaken. I remonstrated that he

9

was building his case on a single verse. His reply was a little sharp: "How many times," he asked, "must God say something to make it true?" This Bible School teacher, so poorly informed on the historic Protestant position regarding interpretation, had completely missed the point. God does not have to say something even once to make it true; he can just think it to himself. But he has to say some things several times before we are sure that we have his meaning. When we wish to proclaim God's Word publicly, or even when we want to decide a question for ourselves, we ought to have as many verses as possible. It is all too easy to misunderstand a statement all by itself. In fact, as is very obvious in discussions on predestination, it is possible to misunderstand a combination of many verses on the same subject. We need not apologize therefore for making so many quotations and treating each one with care.

We were just now talking of God's creation of angels and had quoted Psalm 104:4, 30. There are other verses; we do not depend on this one alone. Psalm 148:5 says, "Let them praise the name of the Lord: for he commanded, and they were created." This "they" includes angels and hosts, sun, moon, and stars, Sun, moon and stars have perhaps been mentioned frequently enough now—if we read the entire first chapter of Genesis and not merely the few lines quoted; but this second reference to angels is a helpful addition. It would be burdensome to continue with all the scriptural passages that assert God's creation of the physical universe. If indeed someone, perhaps a Buddhist or an ignorant college student who has never seen a Bible—and a surprising number of my students in courses in philosophy have never seen or opened a Bible—still doubts that this is what the Bible teaches, let him turn to Nehemiah 9:6, Thou, even thou, art Lord alone; thou hast made heaven, the heaven of heavens, with all their host, the earth, and all things that are therein, the seas, and all that is therein, and thou preservest them all; and the host of heaven worshippeth thee."

Although we shall here leave the creation of the physical universe, another Old Testament reference to the spiritual universe of angels and men will be given. Later something along the same line will be seen in the New Testament. But in the Old we read in Isaiah 42:5, "Thus saith God the Lord, he that created the heavens . . . he that spreadeth forth the earth . . . he that giveth breath unto the people upon it, and spirit to them that walk therein." This refers chiefly to mankind.

As for the angels the Old Testament, with the exception of the verses already quoted, is not so explicit as the New. But there are implicit references to the creation of angels. The vision of Isaiah 6 would hardly make sense if the seraphim were not created beings. Psalm 89:6, where the "sons of the mighty" are angels "in heaven," exalts the Lord above them all. In I Kings 22:19 "all the host of heaven" are his servants standing around his throne, and the Lord sends forth one of his spirits to bring confusion on Ahab. Job 1:6 pictures "the sons of God" and Satan with them standing subserviently before the Lord. Psalm 103:20 says that the angels "do his commandments." Similar passages in which the angels are said to be and are used as God's messengers, ministers, and servants are consistent with the idea that they are created beings; these angelic functions are hardly consistent with the idea that they are beings who exist independently of God.

All the references so far have come from the Old Testament. There is one more before we go to the New Testament. This one is Isaiah 45:7, "I form the light and create darkness: I make peace and create evil: I the Lord do all these things." This is a verse that many people do not know is in the Bible. Its sentiment shocks them. They think that God could not have created evil. But this is precisely what

11

the Bible says, and it has a direct bearing on the doctrine of predestination.

Some people who do not wish to extend God's power over evil things, and particularly over moral evils, try to say that the word evil here means such natural evils as earthquakes and storms. The Scofield Bible notes that the Hebrew word here, RA, is never translated sin. This is true. The editors of that Bible must have looked at every instance of RA in the Old Testament and must have seen that it is never translated sin. But what the note does not say is that it is often translated wickedness, as in Genesis 6:5, "And God saw that the wickedness of man was great in the earth." In fact RA is translated wickedness at least fifty times in the Old Testament; and it refers to a variety of ugly sins. The Bible therefore explicitly teaches that God creates sin. This may be an unpalatable thought to a good many people. But there it is, and everyone may read it for himself. As this becomes a major point in predestination, and forms one of the main objections to the doctrine, we shall discuss it later. But let no one limit God in his creation. There is nothing independent of him.

Now we come to the New Testament. Heretofore the references to creation have been detailed. The writer mentioned this, that, and the other thing that God created. In the New Testament the usual rule is not to mention details, but to make general all-inclusive statements. One reason for this is that the New Testament assumes the truth of what is taught in the Old Testament. There is no need to repeat. Some people act as if, or even definitely assert that, we cannot accept any of the Old Testament unless it is repeated in the New. The correct principle, however, is that we should not discard any of the Old unless told to do so in the New—as for example the ceremonial law. Now, the New Testament says that God created all things.

Acts 17:24 reads, "God . . . made the world and all things

therein." Ephesians 3:9 repeats the idea: "God, who created all things by Jesus Christ." It is reiterated again in Colossians 1:13-16, "his dear Son, . . . who is the image of the invisible God . . . for by him were all things created, that are in heaven, and that are in earth, visible and invisible, whether they be thrones, or dominions, or principalities, or powers: all things were created by him and for him." Two other verses may be added, and these should be enough. Hebrews 3:4 says, "He that built all things is God." And Hebrews 11:3 says, "Through faith we understand that the worlds were framed by the word of God."

Is this not enough to show that God created all things? But we wish to be very thorough, and therefore we shall add a small section on the meaning of the word create.

2. THE MEANING OF CREATE

The verses already adduced show the universal extent of God's creative activity. Since no existing thing is excluded, since the repeated use of "all things" permits no exception, since there is not the faintest hint of something in existence before creation (except God himself, of course), it follows that God did not make or fashion things out of pre-existent materials. A carpenter can take a piece of board and make something out of it; if he does not have anything to work on, there is nothing he can make. But God created all things "out of" nothing. God simply said, "Let there be light," and there was light.

The biblical idea of creation therefore is, to use the traditional phrase, "creation ex nihilo," or "fiat" creation. "Fiat" means, "let it be done." As Psalm 33:9 says, "He spake, and it was done."

Some further evidence of creation ex nihilo is found in the verb create. This is a verb that the Old Testament peculiarly restricts to God, and, with certain special exceptions, that are hardly exceptions at that, never uses of men.

13

Conservative theologians often say that the doctrine of creation ex nihilo cannot be based solely on the meaning of the verb create (BARA). God is sometimes said to have "made" the heavens and the earth. So too, God produced some things not directly out of nothing, but out of the dust of the ground. Of course, God first created the dust of the ground, and Psalm 33:6 says, "By the word of the Lord were the heavens made, and all the host of them by the breath of his mouth."

But if a complete argument cannot be based on the verb create, the usage of BARA in the Old Testament certainly adds evidence in favor of fiat creation. The usage in Genesis has already been shown. Creation is a method of production that uses no pre-existing materials. God created "in the beginning." Nothing preceded.

But there are verses in which the verb BARA is used that do not refer to the original creation in Genesis. For example, Psalm 51:10 says, "Create in me a clean heart, O God." Although this is not creation ex nihilo, it is, according to the teaching of the Scripture, something David could not have done for himself. Only God can give a sinner a clean heart. Because we are preparing for a study of predestination, this idea is important and will be taken up again later. But here let the notion be emphasized by only one or two references. Job 14:4 says, "Who can bring a clean thing out of an unclean? Not one." Consider also Ezekiel 36:25-27, "Then will I sprinkle clean water upon you . . . from all your idols will I cleanse you. A new heart also will I give you . . . and cause you to walk in my statutes." These are things that only God can do. Hence the verb BARA in Psalm 51:10 designates a divine action.

Three or four verses in Isaiah also use the verb BARA to designate an action that only God can do. Isaiah 4:5 reads, "The Lord will create upon every dwelling place of mount Zion . . . a cloud and smoke by day. . . ." Isaiah

57:19 says, "I create the fruit of the lips." And Isaiah 65:17 says, "Behold, I create new heavens and a new earth. . . . Be ye glad and rejoice in that which I create: for, behold, I create Jerusalem a rejoicing."

In one way or another these verses describe actions that only God can do. This seems inherent in the meaning of the verb, even though these actions are not those of the original physical creation in the beginning. So the usage and meaning of the verb create adds evidence to the doctrine of fiat creation or creation ex nihilo.

It is said that this is not always true of BARA and that it sometimes has a man as its subject. At first sight this would seem to weaken the evidence for the peculiar and utterly singular character of God's action. But on second thought there turns out to be not much force in this objection. In Hebrew there is a type of verbal conjugation that is completely foreign to our Western languages. We are accustomed to the distinction between the active and passive voices. Perhaps we can imagine a middle voice as it occurs in Greek. But Hebrew has a system of six or seven different—well, they are not *voices* exactly, but they are sets of forms. The meaning of a verb changes from set to set, and sometimes changes drastically. The verb BARA is that way. Here are five instances.

The first two instances are in Joshua 17:15, 18. "And Joshua answered them, If thou be a great people, then get thee up to the wood country, and cut down (BARA) for thyself there . . . the mountain shall be thine, for it is a wood, and thou shalt cut it down (BARA)." The next two are found in Ezekiel 21:19. "Also, thou son of man, appoint thee two ways, that the sword of the king of Babylon may come: both twain shall come forth out of one land: and choose (BARA) thou a place, choose (BARA) it at the head of the way to the city." The fifth instance is a different translation from that in Joshua, but of similar meaning.

15

Ezekiel 23:47 says, "The company shall stone them with stones, and dispatch (BARA, cut down) them with their swords."

This usage does not weaken the evidence for fiat creation, for one might say that the verb BARA is really two verbs. The meaning "cut down" is so different from and so unrelated to any notion of creation that it simply does not bear on the subject. It is also to be noted, for whatever it might be worth, that this second usage of Bara in its different "voice" is extremely rare. It cannot be tied in with the doctrine of creation.

3. OMNIPOTENCE

Now, by implication, even one instance of creation ex nihilo would require an exercise of omnipotence. No man can make anything at all, no matter how slight, out of nothing. And in understanding predestination, it is necessary to understand the omnipotence of God. The foundation of predestination lies in the being of God. We must know what God is, what his power is, what his position as creator is.

As an introduction to the verses that explicitly mention omnipotence, two sample verses on God's power might well be quoted.

"Lift up your eyes on high, and behold who hath created these things, that bringeth out their host by number; he calleth them all by names by the greatness of his might, for that he is strong in power; not one faileth" (Isa. 40:26).

"Thou art worthy, O Lord, to receive glory and honor and power: for thou hast created all things, and for thy pleasure (or, better, because of thy will) they are and were created" (Rev. 4:11).

Not much comment on these two passages is necessary. The verse from Isaiah stresses God's power. Because of his strength he can control what he has made. The New Testament verse, in the alternate and more accurate translation,

16

bases all the arrangements of the universe on the sovereign will of God. Things are what they are because God made them that way. Therefore, for this reason, the Lord is worthy to receive glory and honor, and power.

Although there is no mention of creation in the following verses, they may be added here for the purpose of emphasizing God's omnipotence. To enforce his Covenant and to assure Abraham that he could do what he promised, God said, "I am the Almighty God" (Gen. 17:1). There are also five other references in Genesis to omnipotence, like that of Genesis 28:3, "God Almighty." Looking back to Genesis, God said to Moses, "I appeared unto Abraham . . . by the name of God Almighty" (Ex. 6:3). Ruth 1:20-21 says, "the Almighty hath dealt very bitterly with me . . . the Almighty hath afflicted me." In the book of Job there are easily thirty references to the Almighty. One is Job 40:2, "the Lord answered Job and said, Shall he that contendeth with the Almighty instruct him?"

Turn now to the New Testament. Revelation 1:8 says, "I am Alpha and Omega . . . saith the Lord, which is, and which was, and which is to come, the Almighty." Here the use of Alpha and Omega is perhaps as good an assertion of God's omnipotence as the word Almighty itself. The phrase "Lord God Almighty" is also found in Revelation 4:8; 11:17; 15:3; 16:7, 21, 22, and an equivalent phrase occurs in Revelation 16:14 and 19:15.

The idea of omnipotence is not restricted to instances of the word Almighty. Revelation 19:6 says, "The Lord God omnipotent reigneth."

Later, other verses more explicitly relating to predestination will be quoted to show God's omnipotence. There can be no question about God's power to predestinate. The extent of predestination will have to be shown by particular verses, for although God had the power to creat a hundred planets around the sun, it seems that he created only ten.

17

So too it is possible that God did not in fact predestinate everything he might have; but whether this is so or not must be determined by examining the pertinent passages. We leave this an open question at the moment. But the conclusion is firm: God could predestinate everything — there is no limit to omnipotence.

4. THE PURPOSE OF CREATION

Even in churches that are Bible centered, not to mention the unbelieving synagogues of Satan, the purpose of creation is a topic that receives little emphasis. Perhaps people think that this purpose is so all-inclusive that there is no use in being specific. After the pastor in his sermon has said that God created all things for his own glory, all he can do is sit down or change the subject.

That God created all things for his own glory is indeed a major point. Hebrews 2:10 does not specifically mention the act of creation, but it says that all things exist for God's sake: "for whom are all things." Another reference to all things is found in Romans 11:36, which says, "For of him, and through him, and to him, are all things." The words "to him" seem to indicate that God is himself the purpose of creation: not of course that creation somehow produces God or that God is its evolutionary end product, but that it is God's gift to himself, as it were: he made it for himself, he gave it to himself, it was created "to him." Then there is the familiar phrase of Psalm 19:1, "The heavens declare the glory of God." It would be foolish to argue that only the heavens and not the earth declare the glory of God. Even if there is here no explicit mention of all things, the sense bears this implication.

There are frequent references to parts of the creation being for the glory of God. Some to a greater degree and some to a lesser degree suggest that all things glorify God. The words "for his name's sake" characterize a number of such

18

references; for example, "The Lord will not forsake his people for his great name's sake" (I Sam. 12:22). More closely associated with the idea of creation is Isaiah 47:7, "I have created him for my glory." This very instructive passage refers to Israel. It mentions how God controls and manages various affairs for Israel's good: for Israel's good, no doubt, but ultimately because this control displays God's own power and glory.

There are certain complications in the question about God's purpose in creation. A purpose relates to a foreseen and intended result. This involves an amount of knowledge. We cannot intend a result about which we know nothing. Conversely, the more we know, the more complicated our purposes become. Therefore it is impossible to say very much about God's purpose in creation without saying something about his knowledge. This subject will be discussed in the next chapter.

With any amount of knowledge, even in the case of mankind, there are purposes of purposes. A college student wants a degree because he needs it to get into medical school; and he studies history and zoology to get his degree. Thus he purposes to study, he purposes to get his degree, he purposes to go to medical school and to become a physician later on. So too we may ask about God's more immediate and his more remote purposes.

So far the verses quoted had to do with God's ultimate purpose. Other verses bearing on God's ultimate purpose are the following. Revelation 1:8, previously quoted to show God's omnipotence, can equally well and perhaps even better be used to support the idea that God himself is the end of his own actions. The verse was, "I am Alpha and Omega." Altogether similar is Isaiah 44:6, "I am the first, I also am the last"; and the same words are found in Isaiah 48:12.

As the words first and Alpha indicate the beginning or

19

original cause, so the words Omega and last indicate the final end. Perhaps this is expressed more clearly in Proverbs 16:4, "The Lord hath made all things for himself."

Further support for this general proposition can be found in those scriptural passages where God himself or God's glory is said to be the intended aim and purpose of some particular event. First Corinthians 11:7 says that "man . . . is the image and glory of God"; and Isaiah 46:13 says, "I will place salvation in Zion for Israel my glory." But if God's glory is the end or purpose of man and the Church, so too it is the end of all that sustains man and makes the Church possible. Since the creation of man is obviously an indispensable step in the formation of the Church, we have a chain of purposes from creation through the Church to God's glory.

What is thus true of man and the Church can as well be seen whenever the Bible reflects on the purpose of God's works of providence. Thus Isaiah 43:7, quoted just above, where the general reference is to Israel collectively, singles out each Israelite individually and assures every one of God's saints of his unchangeable love. Each person has been created for God's glory.

God's operations in conducting and edifying the Church are said to be for his glory, as in Isaiah 60:21, where it says, "Thy people also shall be all righteous . . . that I may be glorified." See also Isaiah 61:3.

In these three passages the general or collective sense and the distributive or individual application are interwoven. With this understanding one can refer to Ephesians 1:5, "Having predestinated us to the adoption of children . . . to the praise of the glory of his grace." Of course the main subject for which all this is preparatory is predestination; but here the verse is used only to show that God's glory, the glory of his grace, is the purpose of creation. The phrase "When he shall come to be glorified in his saints" is found

20

in II Thessalonians 1:10. This notion is frequent in the New Testament. John 15:8, "Herein is my Father glorified, that ye bear much fruit." The Apostle Peter directs us that "if any man speak, let him speak as the oracles of God . . . that God in all things may be glorified." There is a long list of verses in which various particulars are to glorify God, and therefore creation, by which these particulars arise, has this purpose.

If anyone is a little dubious about the general principle's being implicit in the particular examples, and therefore wonders whether the purpose of creation can be seen in the purpose of the Church, there is one most interesting verse that asserts this very thing.

5. CREATION AND THE CHURCH

Ephesians 3:8-10 reads as follows (study it carefully): "Unto me who am less than the least of all saints is this grace given, that I should preach among the Gentiles the unsearchable riches of Christ; and to make all men see what is the fellowship of the mystery, which from the beginning of the world hath been hid in God, who created all things by Jesus Christ, to the intent that now unto the principalities and powers in heavenly places might be known by the church the manifold wisdom of God." Note just as a preliminary step that this passage mentions the preaching of Paul, the creation of the world, and a certain revelation of God's wisdom to heavenly creatures.

The main exegetical problem of this passage, which must be solved in order to understand it aright, is the identification of the antecedent of the purpose clause. Something happened *in order that* the wisdom of God might be made known by means of the Church to heavenly beings, according to God's eternal purpose which he purposed in Christ Jesus our Lord. What was it that happened for this purpose? What is the antecedent of the purpose clause?

21

There are three, and apparently only three, possible antecedents: Paul's preaching might have had this purpose; the mystery was hid for this purpose; or, God created the world for this purpose.

The second of these possibilities is the least likely. We can eliminate it from consideration because this interpretation would hold that God kept a certain secret hidden from the beginning in order to reveal it in New Testament times. The only support in the wording of the verses for this interpretation, aside from the fact that the event of hiding is mentioned prior to the purpose clause, is the word *now*. By emphasizing the word *now*, one may say that the mystery or secret was kept hidden for the purpose of revealing it *now*. It is true that the emphatic position is given to the verb *might be made known*, and hence a contrast with a previous hiding is pointed out. The word *now*, however, is not particularly emphatic and cannot bear the burden of this exegesis. The burden is considerable, for while it is possible to hide something in order to reveal it at a later date, it is more probable that the revelation is the purpose of Paul's preaching or of God's creation of the world. Hiding is more or less a negative idea, and it seems reasonable to expect some definite and outward event that has happened for the purpose stated here.

This is not to deny that there is some minimum truth in the notion that God hid the secret earlier in order to reveal it later. Surely it could not have been revealed later if it had not been hid earlier. But this is a relatively unimportant truth, and the passage has much more to say.

Let us then consider the next possibility. The interpretation that Paul was called to preach in order that God's wisdom might be made known seems to fit in very well with the preceding context.

In verse 8 Paul had just referred to the grace God had given him for the purpose of preaching the Gospel to the

Gentiles. From this point the long complicated sentence continues to the end of verse 13. Even further back, as early as verse 2, the idea of Paul's preaching had been introduced. Therefore no one can doubt that Paul's preaching is the main idea of the passage, or at least one of the main ideas. Whether or not Paul's personal ministry recedes from its central position as the paragraph approaches its end, and what other subordinate ideas may be found in verses 9-11, must of course be determined by direct examination. But the idea of Paul's preaching is without doubt prominent.

The question now is whether or not Paul's preaching has for its stated purpose the revelation of God's wisdom to the powers in heaven. It is obviously true that the purpose of Paul's preaching was to reveal God's wisdom to men on earth. This was both God's purpose and Paul's purpose. But was it God's purpose (it could hardly have been Paul's purpose) to reveal his wisdom to heavenly beings through the preaching of Paul?

Some good commentators think that this is what the passage means. Charles Hodge is one such commentator. Aside from his objection to other interpretations, which we shall study presently, his positive argument is as follows: "The apostle is speaking of his conversion and call to the apostleship. To him was the grace given to preach the unsearchable riches of Christ, and to teach all men the economy of redemption, 'in order that' through the Church might be made known the manifold wisdom of God. It is only thus that the connection of this verse with the main idea of the context is preserved. It is not the design of creation, but the design of the revelation of the mystery of redemption, of which he is here speaking" (*Commentary, in. loc.*, p. 119).

For the moment the only objection to Hodge's exegesis is the seemingly peculiar notion that Paul's preaching on earth reveals the wisdom of God to the powers in heaven.

Paul preached to men; he did not preach to angels, demons, or whomever these powers may be. Admittedly, in the chain of divine intentions and the purposes of purposes, Paul's preaching and the founding of the Church can be said to reveal God's wisdom to these powers, if we suppose that God directed their attention to what was going on; but it would be a purpose two or three steps removed. Immediately it would seem more natural to connect Paul's preaching with its effects on men, rather than on angels or demons.

There is no decisive grammatical reason why Paul's preaching cannot be the antecedent of the purpose clause. Hodge's interpretation is a quite possible meaning of the passage. And, as with the case of the notion of hiding, there is at least a minimum of truth in it. All of God's purposes form a connected system, and in some way a preceding event has for its purpose anything that succeeds it.

On the other hand, there is a third interpretation, also grammatically possible, one that seems to have weightier reasons in its favor, and which does not suffer under the objections raised against it. Grammatically, in fact, this third interpretation is not merely equally good, but somewhat preferable; and it makes better sense out of the passage as a whole.

When we say that God created the world for the purpose of displaying his manifold wisdom, we connect the purpose clause with its nearest antecedent. As anyone can see, the reference to Paul's preaching lies several clauses further back. The immediate antecedent is creation, and this immediate connection between creation and the purpose clause is, we hold, of some value in deciding the matter. It is usually better to choose the nearest possible antecedent.

Since therefore the syntax is at least somewhat in its favor, the best procedure is to examine objections against so understanding it.

The objections are well stated by Charles Hodge. The

24

view that God created the universe in order to display his manifold wisdom is, as Hodge says, the supralapsarian view. Never mind the technical theological name at the moment. Against this view Hodge urges four objections. First, this passage is the only passage in Scripture adduced as directly asserting supralapsarianism, and supralapsarianism, so Hodge says, is foreign to the New Testament. Second, apart from such a doctrinal consideration, this interpretation imposes an unnatural connection on the clauses. The idea of creation in Ephesians 3:10 is entirely subordinate and unessential. It could have been omitted, says Hodge, without materially affecting the sense of the passage. Third, the theme of the passage concerns Paul's preaching the Gospel; only by connecting the purpose clause with Paul's preaching can the unity of the context be preserved. And fourth, the word *now*, in contrast with the previous hiding, supports the reference to Paul's preaching. It was Paul's preaching that had *now* put an end to the secret's hiddenness. Such are Hodge's four objections.

Let us consider the last one first. Admittedly it was Paul's preaching that founded the Church, and the founding of the Church made known God's wisdom to the powers in heaven. The supralapsarian interpretation does not deny that Paul played this important part in God's eternal plan. But even so, Paul's preaching was not the immediate cause of the revelation of God's wisdom. It was the existence of the Church that was the immediate cause. Yet grammar prevents us from saying that the Church was founded in order that God's wisdom might be revealed. It is true that the Church was founded in order to reveal God's wisdom, but this is not what the verse says. Now, if several events occurred, all leading up to this revelation of God's wisdom, including the founding of the Church, Paul's preaching, and of course the death and resurrection of Christ that Paul preached, the word *now* in the verse can-

25

not be used to single out Paul's preaching in contrast with other events mentioned in the passage. This fourth objection is therefore a poor one.

Next, the first objection says that this is the only passage adduced as directly asserting supralapsarianism, and supralapsarianism is foreign to the New Testament. The latter half of this objection is a case of begging the question. If this verse teaches supralapsarianism, then the doctrine is not foreign to the New Testament. We should not assume that the doctrine is foreign to the New Testament and then determine what the verse means. We should first determine what the verse means in order to find out whether or not the doctrine is foreign to the New Testament.

To be sure, if this one verse were indeed the only verse in the Bible with supralapsarian overtones, we would be justified in entertaining some suspicion of this interpretation. Hodge does not say explicitly that this is the only verse; he says it is the only verse adduced as directly asserting supralapsarianism.

Well, really, even this verse does not directly assert the whole complex supralapsarian view. Very few verses in Scripture directly assert the whole of any major doctrine. There is no one verse, for example, that gives us the full doctrine of the Trinity. Therefore we must recognize degrees of directness, partial and even fragmentary assertions of a doctrine. And with this recognition, regularly acknowledged in the development of any doctrine, it is evident that this verse does not stand alone in suspicious isolation.

More of the complete doctrine of supralapsarianism will come to light when in the next chapter we discuss the knowledge of God. The main point of the present discussion is whether or not the purpose of creation was to make known the wisdom of God. All that is required at this point is the avoidance of the assumption that this verse in Ephesians cannot mean this before examining it.

26

Thus we come to objection number two. Hodge claims that the supralapsarian interpretation of this verse imposes an unnatural connection upon the clauses. The idea of creation, he said, is entirely unessential and could have been omitted without materially affecting the sense of the passage.

Does not this objection make it clear that Hodge does not know how to handle the reference to creation? He claims that it is unessential, a chance, thoughtless remark that does not affect the sense of the passage. Such careless writing does not seem to me to be Paul's usual style.

For example, in Galatians 1:1 Paul says, "Paul, an apostle, not from men nor through a man, but by Jesus Christ and God the Father who raised him from the dead." Why now did Paul mention that God had raised Jesus Christ? If it were a chance remark without logical connection with the sense of the passage, a remark intended only to speak of some random aspect of God's glory, Paul could have as well said, God who created the universe. But it is fairly clear that Paul had a conscious purpose in selecting the resurrection instead of the creation. He wanted to emphasize, against his detractors, that he had his apostolic authority from Jesus himself. And Jesus was able personally to give him that authority because he was not dead, but had been raised up by God.

So, as Paul chose the idea of resurrection in Galatians, instead of the idea of creation, he also chose the idea of creation in Ephesians instead of resurrection because the idea of creation contributed some meaning to his thought. Certainly the supralapsarian or teleological interpretation of Ephesians 3:10 accommodates the idea of creation, and contrariwise an interpretation that can find no meaning in these words of the text is a poorer interpretation.

The remaining objection is that only by making Paul's preaching the antecedent of the purpose clause can the

27

unity of the context be preserved. The reverse seems to be the case. Not only does Hodge fail to account for the mention of creation, and thus diminish the unity of the context, but further stress on purpose, running from creation to the present, unifies the passage in a most satisfactory manner.

The supralapsarian or teleological understanding of God's working, that is, the understanding that God works for a purpose, enables us to combine all three of these interpretations, including even the second which in itself has so little in its favor, in a unified and intelligible thought. Since God does everything for a purpose (and this truth will be made more clear in the next chapter) and since whatever precedes in time has in a general way the purpose of preparing for what follows, we may say that God kept the secret hidden in order to reveal it now, and also that Paul preached in order to reveal it now. But if God had not created the world, there would have been no Paul to do the preaching, no Church by which the revelation could be made, and no heavenly powers on which to impress the idea of God's manifold wisdom. Only by connecting the purpose clause with the immediate antecedent concerning creation can a unified sense be obtained from the passage as a whole.

We conclude therefore that this was the purpose of creation.

6. THE MEANING OF GLORY

If it has now been sufficiently shown that the ultimate purpose of creation is the glory of God, this chapter may well conclude with a brief statement as to what glory means. The Hebrew word in the Old Testament and its Greek translation in the New sometimes designate the internal excellence of whatever is said to have that glory.

The Hebrew word in its literal sense means weight or heaviness, greatness or abundance. Its opposite is light.

28

The weight of a thing is its worth; a light thing is worthless. Numbers 21:5 refers to "this light bread." This does not mean, as it would in a modern setting, that the bread was well leavened and properly baked so that it was not heavy or soggy. It means that the bread was so light in weight, there was so little of it, that the people were continually hungry. In I Samuel 18:23 David asks whether Saul's servants thought it a light thing, an unimportant thing, to be a king's son-in-law. Belshazzar in Daniel 5:27 was weighed in the balances and found light. Since light bears these derogatory meanings, heavy is the word for excellence.

That weight or glory designates the essential excellence of something can be seen in Genesis 31:1, which speaks of the glory of riches; so does Esther 5:11. When Job's troubles came upon him he said that God had stripped him of his glory (Job 19:9). There are dozens of such verses.

Now, in addition to internal excellence, the word glory can mean the exhibition of this excellence. The brightness of the sun and stars in I Corinthians 15:41 is not precisely their inward constitution but their outward appearance. Ezekiel 1:28 makes it very clear: "As the appearance of the bow that is in the cloud in the day of rain, so was the appearance of the brightness round about. This was the appearance of the likeness of the glory of the Lord." Isaiah 6:1-3 is a more familiar passage: "I saw the Lord sitting upon a throne, high and lifted up, and his train filled the temple. Above it stood the seraphims . . . and the whole earth is full of his glory." Another verse is Isaiah 60:1-2, "Arise, shine, for thy light is come, and the glory of the Lord is risen upon thee." Again, there are dozens of such verses. (Luke 2:9, Acts 22:11, II Cor. 3:7,18, II Cor. 4:4,6, Heb. 1:3, etc.)

Not inconsistent with these usages of the word glory are the instances in John 17:1,4,5, "The hour is come; glorify thy Son that thy Son also may glorify thee. . . . I have glorified thee on the earth. . . . glorify thou me." And so on through this great chapter.

The purpose then of creation will be, not the production of God's internal and eternal excellence, but the display of his greatness to principalities, to powers, and to mere human beings.

That there is a chain or system of purposes is not to be denied. Indeed these details will be insisted upon in the following chapters. Therefore it is quite, true to say that the purpose of creation, or, better, one purpose of creation was to have Abraham born in Ur and move his family to Palestine. But the purpose, the final purpose, the all inclusive purpose is to display God's excellence. If God's excellence contains knowledge or mysteries, then the purpose of creation is to make these known. These are part of God's glory. If God's excellence contains power, then God raised up Pharaoh for the purpose of displaying his power, not precisely to him, but through him so that God's name might be declared throughout all the earth, as is explicitly stated both in Exodus 9:16 and in Romans 9:17.

The manifold subsidiary purposes are all summed up and comprehended in a single ultimate purpose, the glory of God. It is the revelation of God's excellence, the revelation of God himself. He created the world in order to display his sovereign majesty. He is Alpha and Omega, the first and the last, the beginning and the final and ultimate end. Only by realizing the glory and omnipotence of God can a proper understanding of predestination be achieved.

Chapter Two

OMNISCIENCE

As predestination cannot be understood without an adequate appreciation of God's omnipotence, neither can predestination be understood without a realization of God's omniscience. The reason is that predestination relates to God's purposes and intentions, and these are by definition limited by knowledge. If you or I purpose to buy a box of candy for a friend, we must know the friend, we must know where we can buy it, and how we can take it to him. To be sure, in human affairs this knowledge may turn out not to be knowledge at all. Our friend may have just been killed in an auto accident; or less tragic, the store in which we intended to buy the candy may have gone out of business. But with God these surprises are impossible. In the former case there cannot be intentions without supposed knowledge, and in the latter case there can be no intention without actual knowledge. Since, as just said, predestination is a matter of intention, we must consider the extent of God's knowledge.

In the previous chapter, where the aim was to show that God created all things, the first step was to indicate that God had created this, and next that, and so on until we exhausted the list and could conclude that God created all things. Here too one could list the items that the Bible says God knows, and finally conclude that he knows all things. This procedure has some advantages. I had a devout and humble aunt, who when a girl had served a term as a missionary to the Mormons. Years later she advanced some theological opinions to her young nephew. God, she said, took care of the important things in the world, and even was attentive to the work of a young missionary; but God does not know what I am doing in my kitchen, she said, for this is too insignificant for him to notice. Undoubtedly this was humility; she did not think of herself more highly than she should. But her Arminian concept of God was far from what the Bible teaches. Humble she was; but she was humiliating God by supposing that he was so limited in his span of attention that he could not attend both to the important things and to the unimportant things as well. If, now, we should list the things the Bible says God knows, we could find out whether he knows what women do when they are in their kitchens.

But there is a better way to proceed, and the details will fall into place just the same. The procedure will be to show how the doctrine of creation relates to God's knowledge, and how omnipresence and providence relate. With this information the nature of God's knowledge can then be discussed.

1. CREATION, OMNIPRESENCE, AND PROVIDENCE

There is a story about a visitor to Henry Ford's auto plant in the early days. Mr. Ford himself escorted the visitor around. They stopped a moment to watch a foreman work on some interesting procedure. The visitor with Mr. Ford's obvious approval asked the foreman some questions, which he answered satisfactorily. Then the visitor asked, How many separate parts are needed to complete a car? The foreman with slight disgust replied that he could think of no piece of information more useless. Mr. Ford moved on and quietly said, There are 927 (or whatever the number was) pieces.

If now a human inventor and manufacturer has an accurate knowledge of his product, is it surprising that the divine artificer should have an even more accurate knowledge of what he has made? Since God has created all things, we infer that God has a perfect knowledge of all his creation.

Though this is so plausible in itself, we need not rely on Mr. Ford for our theology. Analogies are sometimes deceptive, and we always need Scripture. There is Scripture to cover this point. In Psalm 139:2, 15, 16 David acknowledges that God knows him because God made him. The verses have other implications too, but here attention is directed to the idea that David was made, fashioned, curiously wrought, and all his members were catalogued. The verses are: "Thou knowest my downsitting and mine uprising, thou understandest me though afar off. . . . My substance was not hid from thee, when I was made in secret, and curiously wrought in the lowest parts of the earth. . . . Thine eyes did see my substance, yet being unperfect; and in thy book all my members were written, which in continuance were fashioned, when as yet there was none of them."

Take another verse. Psalm 104:24 says, "O Lord, how manifold are thy works! in wisdom hast thou made them all." The construction of the parts of the universe is incredibly intricate, far more so than a Model T Ford. The wisdom and knowledge exhibited in these manifold works are beyond our imagination. Creation is then evidence of God's omniscience. The same idea is found in many other verses. For example, Proverbs 3:19 says, "The Lord by wisdom hath founded the earth; by understanding hath he established the heavens. By his knowledge the depths are broken up." Again, Jeremiah 10:12 reads, "He hath made the earth by his power, he hath established the world by his wisdom, and hath stretched out the heavens by his discretion." No doubt there are dozens of such verses.

These should be enough to show that the doctrine of creation presupposes the doctrine of divine omniscience. If some humble missionary aunt denies the latter, she must in consistency deny the former.

Next comes the idea of omnipresence. There may be some verse in the Bible that speaks only of God's omnipresence; but all the others combine it with some other doctrine. Therefore, instead of giving a separate proof of the former, we shall combine omnipresence and omniscience in one set of references. The two omni's go together.

The prophet Jeremiah says, "Can any hide himself in secret places that I shall not see him? saith the Lord. Do not I fill heaven and earth?" (23:24). The reason that no one can escape the attention of God is that God is everywhere. He fills heaven and earth. What is present to him, he knows. And while the verse mentions only human beings who might wish to hide from him, the implication is that God knows everything because he is everywhere.

Although we often say that God is everywhere in the world, it might better be said that the world everywhere is in God. Acts 17:24-28 refers to creation, omnipresence, and by implication knowledge when it says, "God that made the world and all things therein . . . dwelleth not in temples made with hands"; and then when it adds that "in him we live and move and have our being," we can infer that the "all things" of the earlier verse also have their being in God. Obviously God must know whatever is thus present to him or thus in his mind.

The well-known verses of Psalm 139 use the idea of omnipresence to enforce a lesson concerning God's knowledge. "Whither shall I go from thy spirit . . . if I make my bed in hell, thou art there." Not only in hell, but if I fry bacon and eggs in the kitchen, "even there shall thy hand lead me, and thy right hand shall hold me."

The same combination of ideas is found also in Hebrews

4:13, "Neither is there any creature that is not manifest in his sight; but all things are naked and opened unto the eyes of him with whom we have to do."

As omnipresence and creation support omniscience, so also does providence. Creation and providence are combined in Nehemiah 9:6, where the next to the last phrase is, "Thou preservest them all." Psalm 36:6 reads, "O Lord, thou preservest man and beast." Speaking particularly about creeping things and beasts both small and great, Psalm 104:27 continues, "These wait all upon thee, that thou mayest give them their meat in due season." Other verses on providence will later be used more closely in conjunction with predestination; but here only one will now be added. In Matthew 6:32 Jesus says, "Your heavenly Father knoweth that ye have need of all these things."

This last verse which ties providence to knowledge is most appropriate. How could God exercise providence over all his creation unless he knew it all? Since the providence of God concerns the particulars of life, God must know these particulars. The word providence refers to God's governance and control of the conditions under which man and beast and creeping things live; but etymologically providence is a matter of seeing or knowing.

If God's governance of the world covers the distribution of eternal rewards and eternal punishment, though no verses will be quoted on this right here, and if merit and sin depend in part on the thoughts and intentions of the heart, that is, on men's secret motivations, then this governance depends on God's knowledge of men's inmost thoughts. The Apostle tells us that "the Lord . . . will bring light to the hidden things of darkness and will make manifest the counsels of the hearts" (I Cor. 4:5). All such considerations enforce the doctrine of omniscience.

An example of this is Peter's confession, "Lord, thou knowest all things, thou knowest that I love thee" (John

21:17). This verse is particularly to the point. Christ knows Peter's heart because he knows all things. The condition of Peter's love was not just some accidental bit of information that Jesus happened to have. Jesus was Lord, Jehovah, God, and he knew Peter's love because he was omniscient. With this one may compare John 2:24-25, "He knew all men, and needed not that anyone should testify of man, for he knew what was in man." These last two quotations are often used to prove the deity of Christ; but note that they do so on the basis that God is omniscient.

2. SHORT SUMMARY

The various considerations now set forth can be summarized and enforced by other verses of general application. The Scriptures teach that God is a God of knowledge. The words of I Samuel 2:3 are, "The Lord is a God of knowledge, and by him actions are weighed." Psalm 147:5 says, "Great is the Lord, and of great power: his understanding is infinite."

In case a reader think that all this belabors the obvious, it is to be noted that some ministers and theologians have become so confused about predestination that they have denied omniscience. It may be that later on this reader will be tempted to suppose that there are some things God does not and cannot know. Attributing ignorance to God enables us to escape some objections to predestination; but this escape costs the sovereignty, the omniscience, the wisdom, even the deity of God. Therefore the purpose of "belaboring the obvious," of heaping up the scriptural material on God's knowledge, is to prevent any such disastrous misunderstanding of predestination. The reader should ask himself, Does not the preceding material, plus the details about to follow, show fully and completely that God knows everything?

It is hard to say whether people who have difficulty with

36

predestination are more troubled with God's foreknowledge of the thoughts and intents of man's heart or with his knowledge of non-human details. The latter are not so important to us as the former, but nevertheless one paragraph at least should be inserted somewhere to show God's knowledge of inanimate particulars. One such item is God's knowledge of the starry host of heaven. This knowledge is mentioned several times in the Bible. For example, God brought Abraham into the open and said, "Look now toward heaven, and tell the stars, if thou be able to number them" (Gen. 15:5). What Abraham could not do (for Jeremiah 33:22 says, "The host of heaven cannot be numbered" by man at any rate) God can do, for "He telleth the number of the stars; he calleth them all by their names" (Psalm 147:4). To this verse, add "He calleth them all by names by the greatness of his might, for that he is strong in power" (Isaiah 40:26).

It is interesting to note in this last phrase that God's knowledge seems dependent on his power. In the next subsection on the nature of God's knowledge, this will be discussed. At the moment it is sufficient to end this short summary by concluding that the Bible most clearly teaches that God knows all things.

3. THE NATURE OF GOD'S KNOWLEDGE

In the discussion on providence, just above, it was said that the word etymologically refers to seeing things, and more definitely refers to seeing things ahead of time. John 6:64 says, "But there are some of you that believe not; for Jesus knew from the beginning who they were that believed not, and who should betray him." The phrase "from the beginning" might mean only from the time these people began to follow him. Or, it might mean from the beginning of man's history. Or it might mean from eternity, in the same sense in which the Apostle says, "In the beginning was the

Word." Since the Old Testament prophesies that Christ should be betrayed, it would seem that this knowledge antedated Judas' birth. When compared with other verses, this one most probably means that Jesus knew from all eternity. God's knowledge is eternal.

If God's knowledge were not eternal, then he must have learned something at some time. And if he learned it, he must have previously been ignorant of it. And if he had been ignorant and learned something, why could he not forget some things after a while?

However, God neither learns nor forgets. "He that keepeth Israel shall neither slumber nor sleep" (Psalm 121:4). I Corinthians 2:11 says, "What man knows the things of a man save the spirit of man which is in him? even so the things of God knoweth no man, but the Spirit of God." This verse indicates, what is otherwise not surprising, that God knows himself; and if God is eternal and uncreated, the original Self Existent, then his knowledge of himself must be eternal.

The phrase that refers to God as "declaring the end from the beginning" (Isa. 46:10), and the verse "Known unto God are all his works from the beginning of the world" (Acts 15:18) indicate the eternity of divine knowledge. If anyone should insist that the words "from the beginning of the world" push back God's knowledge only to the date of creation, a reply has already been noted in God's knowledge of himself and in his eternal freedom from ignorance. Another reply will be given at the beginning of the next chapter.

Perhaps a verse should be included to show that God is eternal. If he were not eternal, then of course his knowledge would not be eternal. Now, the doctrine of creation ex nihilo presupposes the eternity of God, but a particular verse is "The high and lofty One that inhabiteth eternity" (Isa. 57:15); as also Genesis 21:33, "the everlasting God";

38

Psalm 90:2, "even from everlasting to everlasting thou art God"; Psalm 102:26-27, "They shall perish . . . but thou art the same, and thy years shall have no end"; and I Timothy 1:17, "the King eternal."

At the end of the last sub-section there was a verse connecting God's knowledge with his power. He knows because he is omnipotent. In fact, there are several verses that connect God's knowledge and his power. This is to be expected if we keep in mind that God and his power are eternal. When as yet there was nothing, and only God existed, God knew all things. Obviously this knowledge came out of or resided in himself. He could not have derived it from anything else, for there was nothing else. It was really self-knowledge, for his knowledge of the universe was his knowledge of his own intentions, his own mind, his own purposes and decisions.

In philosophical language this means that God's knowledge is not empirical. He does not discover the truth. He always has the truth. The point is rather important, and it has important bearings on predestination. Let us say it over again for one more paragraph.

If God is indeed as the Bible describes him, with eternal self-knowledge, by which he creates and controls every particular in the world, obviously God's knowledge depends on himself and not on created things. God's knowledge is self-originated; he does not learn from any outside source. Note that Proverbs 8:22 says, "The Lord possessed me from the beginning of his way." And the idea is repeated and reinforced in the immediately following verses. This shows that God did not learn about me from observing me. It does not say that God knows me from the beginning of my way, but from the beginning of his way. So too Isaiah 40:13 says, "Who hath directed the Spirit of the Lord, or being his counsellor hath taught him? With whom took he counsel and who instructed him . . . and taught him knowledge."

Therefore God is the source of his omniscience. He does not learn from things: his knowledge depends on himself alone and is as eternal as he is.

4. STEPHEN CHARNOCK

There is now a more efficient way to pursue the question of the nature of God's knowledge. A great Puritan writer, Stephen Charnock, wrote a tremendously long volume on *The Existence and Attributes of God.* Though it will be impossible to reproduce all he said on the Knowledge of God, some selections from chapters VIII and IX will carry the discussion forward and at the same time give us an example of Puritan theology.

Charnock says, "God knows himself because his knowledge with his will is the cause of all other things; . . . he is the first truth, and therefore is the object of his understanding. . . . As he is all knowledge so he hath in himself the most excellent object of knowledge. . . . No object is so intelligible to God as God is to himself, . . . for his understanding is his essence, himself" (Vol. I, p. 415, ed. 1873). Then a few pages later: "God knows his own decree and will, and therefore must know all future things. . . . God must know what he hath decreed to come to pass . . . God must know because he willed them . . . he therefore knows them because he knows what he willed. The knowledge of God cannot arise from the things themselves, for then the knowledge of God would have a cause without him. . . . As God sees things possible in the glass of his own power, so he see things future in the glass of his own will" (*ibid.,* p. 433).

The quotation from Charnock mentions a knowledge of things possible. This is an additional idea that deserves a little explanation. With merely a general knowledge of Scripture one might suppose that God knows what he could have done, but did not. It would be queer to say that God

40

knows the actual planets around the sun, but does not know what other planets he might have created. Yet let us not be satisfied with merely a general knowledge of Scripture, the residue of a vague memory of previous reading. Romans 4:17 says, "God . . . calleth those things which be not as though they were." I Corinthians 1:28 adds, ". . . hath God chosen, yea, and things which are not, to bring to nought things that are." What God calls and chooses is not unknown to him. Thus he knows what is possible, whether or not he ever makes it actual.

5. NUMEROUS DETAILS

God also knows what is impossible. Since he knows himself, he knows that he cannot lie. This "inability" is not a limit on his omnipotence; it merely means that whatever God declares is ipso facto true. To say that God can lie is as much a misunderstanding of the nature of God as to say that a triangle has only two sides is a misunderstanding of the nature of a triangle.

For the purpose of studying predestination it may not be so necessary to insist on God's knowledge of the possible as it is to insist on his knowledge of what is or will be actual. The reason is that predestination has to do with what God intends and purposes.

What he does not purpose cannot come to pass, because the world is made according to the divine omniscience of foreknowledge.

Let us continue therefore to note how explicitly and in detail the Scripture asserts God's knowledge of what is or will be actual. These two divisions are both found in Scripture, and indeed are found together in one verse. When the Lord challenges the idols and their makers in Isaiah 41:22, he says, "Let them . . . show us what shall happen: let them show the former things . . . or declare us things for to come." The force of the challenge lies in the fact that

41

the idols know neither the past nor the future, while God knows both.

As for things past it was necessary that God should know them in order to reveal, for instance, the stages of creation and the events in Eden to Moses many centuries later. We could hardly suppose that the circumstances of Cain's murder of Abel, much less the sentiments of Lamech in Genesis 4:19-24, could have been handed down to the time of Moses by word of mouth. But if anyone should seriously entertain this possibility, God still would have had to assure Moses that the tradition was accurate. As for Genesis 1:1-25, if there were any tradition, God would have had to know and reveal these past events in order to start the tradition.

Knowledge of the past underlies Ecclesiastes 3:15, "That which has been is now, and that which is to be hath already been; and God requireth that which is past."

Other verses which assert God's knowledge of past, present, future, or all three, are: Genesis 1:18, 21, 25, 31, "God saw everything that he had made, and behold it was very good." Psalm 50:11 says, "I know all the fowls of the mountains, and the wild beasts of the field are mine." God knows all the actions of men, for Job 31:4 says, "Doth not he see my ways and count all my steps?" It would be foolish to suppose that God knew only Job's steps, and not Adam's, Paul's, yours and mine. Even if this were so, it would still imply that God foreordained all of Job's steps; and this has considerable weight in connecting foreordination with tragedies. In addition to Job, David would also have to be included, for Psalm 56:8 says, "Thou tellest my wanderings; put thou my tears into thy bottle; are they not in thy book?" Here the Scripture asserts that God knew and knows what David did; even his tears are kept in the divine memory. Not only are Job and David known to God, but the foolishness of not extending God's knowledge to all men is seen

42

in Proverbs 5:21, "For the ways of man [all men] are before the eyes of the Lord, and he pondereth all his goings." God is not ignorant of even a single thing that any man does. This verse in Proverbs is completely general and includes all the actions of men that are still future to us.

Similarly when the Lord says, "The very hairs of your head are all numbered" (Matt. 10:30), he implies knowledge of the past and the future. The statement is not intended to be limited just to those Jews who actually heard his words at that time and place. It is a perfectly general assertion of God's knowledge of all details at all times and in all places.

The same is true of Luke 22:11. Jesus knew that "when ye are entered into the city, there shall a man meet you bearing a pitcher of water . . . and he shall show you a large upper room furnished." It is true that in our every day lives we often say, "Go to the store and you will find Mrs. Smith at the cosmetic counter," without our claiming omniscience. But our predictions sometimes fail. Mrs. Smith may have met with an accident that morning and will be in the hospital instead of at the counter. The store may even have dropped its cosmetic line and no such counter will be there. But Jesus' prediction, like all the other prophecies, often made centuries in advance, is based on a knowledge of all details so that there is no possibility that the man did not find a pitcher that day or fail to fill it with water. God knew not only that the pitcher and the water were available; he also knew that the man would choose to fill the pitcher and carry it at the given time and place. "He discerns the thoughts and intents of the heart" (Heb. 4:12). "Hell and destruction are before him, much more then the hearts of the children of men" (Prov. 15:11). God told Elisha, and therefore must have known, the secret plans of the King of Syria (II Kings 6:12). "Thou understandest my thoughts afar off" (Ps. 139:2).

To mention further particulars, implied in the previous verses and explicitly stated in others, God knows the sins of every man. In Job 11:11, Zophar says, "He knoweth vain men, he seeth wickedness also." If someone suggest that we cannot accept Zophar's words as indubitably true, for at the end of the book God declares that Job's comforters have not spoken well, nevertheless Psalm 14:2-3 says, "The Lord looked down from heaven upon the children of men to see if there were any that did understand and seek God. [But] they are all gone aside, they are all together become filthy: there is none that doeth good, no not one." When David says "Cleanse thou me from secret faults," he implies that God knows them, for otherwise God could not cleanse him. He knows these sins before they are committed. In Deuteronomy 31:20, 21 God says, "When I shall have brought them into the land . . . that floweth with milk and honey . . . then will they turn unto other gods and serve them . . . and break my covenant. . . . for I know their imagination [intentions] which they go about, even now, before I have brought them into the land."

The last verse for this chapter is Genesis 50:20. After Joseph's brethren had sold him into slavery and had later rediscovered him as the second ruler in Egypt, and after their father Jacob had died, they were afraid that Joseph would take vengeance upon them. Joseph replied, "As for you, ye thought evil against me, but God meant it unto good." God knew all the sins of Joseph's brothers, and he also knew long before it happened that good would result from these sins.

Did God merely know these sins ahead of time, or did he predestinate and foreordain them? All this insistence on God's knowledge, God's knowledge of all things, God's knowledge of all sins, centuries before they occurred, from eternity in fact, is preparation for the proper understanding of predestination. As will be seen, some who think they are

Bible students get so confused with predestination and objections against this doctrine, that they have taken the extreme step of denying that God is all knowing. Surely enough has already been given to rule out such an impious refuge from the biblical doctrine of predestination.

Yet this impious refuge has some consistency to it. Whether or not God foreordains sinful acts, this chapter has made abundantly clear that he knows these sinful acts from all eternity. This knowledge of the future is not the same as alleged human knowledge of the future. We may say carelessly that we know it will rain tomorrow. We really do not know. We may have a plausible opinion that it will rain; but since our plausible opinions are several times mistaken, we cannot say that we really know. But God knows. He does not entertain a merely plausible opinion that may turn out to be mistaken. What he knows always happens. When Cain killed Abel, God knew that Joseph's brothers would sell him into slavery. This evil act was therefore inevitable. It could not not-happen. Foreknowledge implies inevitability. If Joseph's brothers had killed him, as they first thought of doing, then God would have been mistaken. The sale had to take place. Does this mean that God foreordains sinful acts? Well, it surely means that these acts were certain and determined from all eternity. It means that the brothers could not have done otherwise. Then who made those acts certain? The brothers could not have made them certain, for they were not yet born at the time of Cain and Abel. If God did not determine them, then there must be in the universe a determining force independent of God. You can escape this conclusion simply by denying that God knows all things.

This simple escape is simply an escape from God and the Bible. The verses selected for this chapter are only a few that could have been used to show that God knows everything; but they are more than enough to make the point.

No one can now deny that the Bible teaches God's omniscience. But as has just slightly been seen in the last paragraph, these verses yield further implications, which with the help of additional passages will take us the next step on our way. It has to do with God's eternal decree.

Chapter Three

THE ETERNAL DECREEE AND ITS EXECUTION

This chapter may well begin by repeating a verse previously quoted. Acts 15:17-18 reads, ". . . saith the Lord who doeth all these things. Known unto God are all his works from the beginning of the world." Instead of this, the American Revision of 1901 substitutes, "saith the Lord, who maketh these things known from of old." The King James version is based on what is generally thought to be an inferior text; but the American Revision is a doubtful translation. In the face of these defects the passage needs a moment's study.

The occasion is the Jerusalem Council. Immediately prior to the gathering Paul and Barnabas "declared all things that God had done with them," chiefly with respect to the conversion of the Gentiles. When some of the Pharisees opposed Paul, the council convened and Peter defended Paul. After some general dabate James gave the decision. He declares that the inclusion of the Gentiles had been prophesied by Amos. The last phrase in Amos is "saith the Lord that doeth this"; in James's mouth the word *this* becomes "these things." Now, the American Revision must be mistaken when it says, "the Lord maketh these things known." The sense, as is clear from Amos, is that the Lord "makes" or does these things. That is, the Lord converted the Gentiles. These things, however, were "known" of old. The word "known" is not the object of the verb make or do, which in fact is only a participle; the word "known" is adjectival to "these things." A literal translation is, "saith the Lord doing these things, known of old."

But who knew these things of old? Hardly Amos. Most of the Christians who saw these things happening did not understand them. Amos even less. It was God who knew. But to say that God knew these things from of old, say, from the time of Moses, or even Adam, is an incongruous suggestion. In addition to such a temporally limited reference, the words can equally well be translated "from eternity," and this is what the sense of the verse requires.

1. God Plans and Acts

This verse, then, says that God plans and acts. Perhaps it does not quite say that God plans. It only says that God knows. But who can deny that God plans? Although the title of the book is *Biblical Predestination*, and the aim is to heap up as many verses as possible, it may be excusable not to insert here a list of all the prophecies recorded in the Old Testament. Anyone can think of a dozen of them. Many of the prophecies say explicitly that God will do this or that. In one place God said to Abraham, "I will make thee exceeding fruitful, and I will make nations of thee." In a prior chapter God predicts the slavery of the Israelites in Egypt and says, "that nation, whom they shall serve, I will judge." In both of these places God declares his plan and purpose. It is not merely a prediction that something will happen somehow, but a statement that God will do it. Therefore God plans these events. What is explicit here is implicit in all the prophecies. All of them mean that God acts and plans what he will do. And then he does it. God plans and acts.

In the eighteenth century a form of religion called Deism was popular. The Deists believed in God, a sort of God, who did nothing. He may have created the world in the beginning, but then he sat back and let nature and history progress under their own laws and forces. Miracles never happened; prayer was useless; divine intervention was impossible. Deism as a movement disintegrated in the nineteenth century; but its varieties, called by other names, continue to exist. Among those who accept a good bit of the Bible, who accept miracles and the Resurrection, a form of Deism persists in the notion that even if God knows all things, still he does not do or cause all things. For example, God perhaps knew that Judas would betray Christ, but he did not cause or predestine Judas to do so. He just sat back and let Judas follow his own laws and inclinations. But is this deistic view of divine causality biblical? One must now ask, what limits, if any, does the Bible impose on God's activity?

To list the instances of God's activity by enumerating everything he has done would require a repetition of the whole Bible. God created the world, he created Adam, he formed Eve from Adam's rib, he drove them from the garden of Eden, and he sent the flood. Obviously an enumeration would take us all the way from Genesis to Revelation. But out of this great mass of material certain important points can be chosen to give us a proper understanding of the sphere of God's activity. We want to know whether or not God did all these things deliberately and on purpose. Or instead of acting, did he merely react to some unexpected and unpleasant interruptions? What is the extent of his plan and the extent of its execution? First, some Old Testament passages will be chosen, and later some New Testament passages.

The first four references are very general in scope. The first two are not only identical in thought; they are almost identical in wording. Psalm 115:3 says, "Our God is in the heavens: he hath done whatsoever he hath pleased." And Psalm 135:6 says, "Whatsoever the Lord pleased, that did he in heaven and in earth, in the seas, and all deep places."

No one is surprised to hear that the Lord pleased to deliver the children of Israel from Egypt, and he did so. But one might at first be surprised to hear that it pleased the Lord to enslave those people for two centuries or more before delivering them. But since the Lord does whatsoever he pleases, it follows inexorably that it did not please him to prevent their slavery or to deliver them sooner than he did. Take any example that comes to mind: the destruction of Jerusalem in 588 B.C., the destruction of Jerusalem in A.D. 70, the sack of Rome in A.D. 410, the wars of Napoleon, Wilhelm II, and Hitler. Had God pleased, these things would not have happened, for God does everything he pleases. At the very least, we must say that God was pleased to let history occur as it has occurred.

But we can say more. The next reference not only repeats the previous idea, but adds to it. It is a verse, part of which has already been quoted. Isaiah 46:10 says, "Declaring the end from the beginning, and from ancient times the things that are not yet done, saying, my counsel shall stand, and I will do all my pleasure." The first phrase about the end from the beginning reflects on the eternity of God's knowledge. This needs no further emphasis. The phrase, "my counsel shall stand," contains an idea that needs emphasis at this point. How extensive is God's counsel? Counsel means design or plan. What does this design or purpose include? Does anything escape it? Here the section on omniscience should be recalled. God knows everything. He must, if he is to provide for every beast and creeping thing. He must, if he is to bring to pass the many prophecies recorded. A change of dynasty was needed to enslave the Israelites in Egypt. Judas and Pontius Pilate had to be born in a certain century, and therefore their parents had to marry at a given time; and for this many other conditions had to be satisfied, and these conditions depended on remoter events. The fulfilment of any one prophecy requires control of the whole universe, lest something prevent its occurrence. When then God says, My counsel shall stand, he asserts omniscient and omnipotent control. This is his pleasure. He has arranged things so. He did not merely look ahead and see what would happen independently of him. Nothing is independent of him. He created all things. Thus the course of history from the past on to the things that are not yet done are parts of God's plan; and God, declaring the end from the beginning, says, my counsel, my plan, my decree shall stand, and I shall do all my pleasure. Nothing that God wants done is left undone. If God had not wanted Jerusalem destroyed, he would have prevented it. Clearly he wanted it destroyed.

The last of these four verses is equally general in scope, equally decisive in clarity, and a little bit more explicit. Daniel 4:35 says, "All the inhabitants of the earth are reputed as nothing: and he doeth according to his will in the army of heaven, and among the inhabitants of the earth: and none can stay his hand, or say unto him, what doest thou?"

The first phrase of this verse shows that human desires and preferences cannot be urged as objections to God's intentions. Not only were the desires of Pharaoh irrelevant to the escape of the Israelites, but the pious hopes of Jeremiah could not deter God from destroying Jerusalem. It is true, and the truth is important, that God uses men in his plans. God used Jeremiah; but he used him to increase the guilt of the wicked kings and false prophets. Yet Jeremiah in himself and all the inhabitants of the earth together are reputed as nothing. The world and the course of history were not planned ultimately for them, but for the glory of God. Since this is so, and because of his omnipotence, God doeth according to his will and decree both in heaven and earth; and none can stay his hand. Because God willed to destroy Jerusalem and decreed to overthrow the Roman Empire, no imperial and military energy could stay his hand. By God's decision it was inevitable, unavoidable, unpreventable, necessary, and irresistible that the barbarians should plunge Europe into a period of Dark Ages and that not only Belshazzar, but several presidents of the United States also should be murdered. Some people may not like all this, but no one can stay God's hand nor even complain by saying, what doest thou?

These verses have been completely general in scope. God controls everything. He does whatever he pleases. The next two verses point particularly to one single event, but in such a way that the universal scope of God's action is made clear. The first of these is also from Daniel. Daniel 11:36 says, "And the king . . . shall speak marvellous things against the God of gods, and shall prosper till the indignation be accomplished: for that that is determined shall be done." This verse refers to a wicked king who should prosper for a time, "till the indignation be accomplished." Then a particular event, presumably including the destruction of this king, is to take place. This event was predetermined, and that is why its occurrence is certain. The event is a particular, individual event, but its certainty is based on the principle that whatever is determined shall be done.

The second verse refers to a different event, but the implications are identical. Job 23:13-14 says, "He is in one mind, and who can turn him? and what his soul desireth, even that he doeth. For he performeth the thing that is appointed for me." Here Job acknowledges that God cannot be turned from the series of events which he has planned. Whatever God desires, that he does. This may mean that Job must suffer, for God will do to Job what God appointed or decreed for Job. As in Daniel, so here the certainty of the particular event depends on the fact that God determined it. This principle applies no more to the event Job has in mind or the event Daniel has in mind than it applies to every event from the beginning to the end.

2. GOD DETERMINES HUMAN DECISIONS

The material above shows clearly that God plans, decrees, and controls all events. The world goes on just as God pleases. This general principle is logically sufficient to justify predestination. But emphasis on one type of event seems psychologically required. The trouble is that some people concede that God controls large historical trends, and yet at the same time fail to understand that this requires control of human decisions. This illogical quirk leads these people to deny that God decrees and causes each individual choice. But the Bible is not only explicit; its examples are numerous. First, some Old Testament verses will be quoted.

Deuteronomy 2:30 says, "Sihon king of Heshbon would not let us pass by him: for the Lord thy God hardened his spirit, and made his heart obstinate, that he might deliver him into thy hand." But wait a minute.

Someone, reading over the previous verses, might wish to remark that God does not cause the events there referred to, but that he merely permits them to happen. Such a remark ignores God's omnipotence and sovereignty. It presupposes that there is some force in the universe independent of God; no doubt God could counteract this force, but he does not; and the force or agent causes some event entirely apart from God's causation. Now, it is true that Daniel 11:36 does not say explicitly that it was God who determined what should be done. Yet who else could? It is also true that Isaiah does not say explicitly that God does everything: Isaiah merely says God does everything he wants to. So also, when Job 23:13-14 says that the Lord "performeth the thing that is appointed for me," there is no explicit assertion that God appoints and does everything for everybody. But how could it be otherwise, if the verses are to fit into the general argument of their context?

What troubles certain Christians is the idea that God causes evil events. Some Christians even want to withdraw some good events from God's power. When Dr. Billy Graham preached in Indianapolis, I went to hear him. Toward the end of the service he asked people to come forward and a crowd came. With them before him evangelist Graham addressed the large audience still in their seats and delivered a five or ten minute diatribe against Presbyterianism. Don't pray for these people who have come forward, he said. You may have prayed for them before, and that is good. You can pray for them later on, and that will be good too. But right now prayer is useless, for not even God can help them. They must accept Christ of their own free will, all by themselves, and God has no power over the will of man.

Of course, this is full-fledged Arminianism. But most Christians are more perturbed about God's causing evil events. The first verse of this sub-section says explicitly that God hardened the heart of Sihon, king of Heshbon.

Perhaps Pharaoh should have been used for this point. When Pharaoh is mentioned, some people grudgingly admit that the Bible says God hardened his heart, but make the quick comeback that the Bible also says Pharaoh hardened his own heart. This, however, is not very effective as a comeback. Admittedly God often acts through human instrumentalities. The important question therefore is whether or not God is the cause of these instruments. Now, in the book of Exodus the hardening of Pharaoh's heart is mentioned eighteen times, plus one more verse that applies to the Egyptians in general. Exodus 4:21; 7:3, 13; 9:12; 10:1, 20, 27; 11:10; 14:4, 8 all say that the Lord hardened Pharaoh's heart. The extra verse says the Lord hardened the hearts of the Egyptians (Ex. 14:17). This is eleven times out of nineteen. In Exodus 7:14, 22; 8:19; 9:7, 35 no explicit mention of who hardened Pharaoh's heart is made. This is five times. The other verses, three in number, 8:15, 32; and 9:34 say that Pharaoh hardened his heart. Who then, in the face of eleven statements that the Lord hardened Pharaoh's heart can deny that God is the cause of this hardening? Not only is this statement made three times as often; but it is made three times before the other statement is made even once. After all, who runs Egyptian affairs, Pharaoh or God? Naturally Pharaoh also hardened his own heart, for God often uses human instrumentalities in certain situations. But the ultimate, original, and first cause is God.

Now, after this digression on the parallel case of Pharaoh, we can return to the less-well-known case of Sihon, king of Heshbon, whose spirit the Lord made obstinate for the purpose of delivering him into the hands of Moses. We can indeed return to the verse, Deuteronomy 2:30, but we can hardly say anything further, except that there is no statement that Sihon hardened his own heart. The immediate conclusion therefore is that the hardening of human hearts is within the scope of divine activity.

Later on in the Bible I Samuel 16:14 says, "But the Spirit of the Lord departed from Saul, and an evil spirit from the Lord troubled him." This verse indicates that Saul's previous policies, victories, and successes in unifying Israel had been accomplished through the Spirit of the Lord. The Holy Spirit had given him wisdom and strength. Now the Holy Spirit leaves Saul. At the moment no inquiry will be made into the question whether Saul had been regenerate and was from this point on unregenerate. The Holy Spirit may dwell with a man, especially a divinely selected king of Israel, with several results. What is clear here is that the Lord sent a spirit to Saul to trouble or terrify him. That this is not an altogether singular occurrence will be seen in the next verse.

In I Kings 22:20-23 the inspired author writes, "The Lord said, who shall persuade Ahab that he may go up and fall at Ramoth-gilead. . . . And there came forth a spirit and stood before the Lord and said, I will persuade him. . . . I will be a lying spirit in the mouth of all his prophets. And he [the Lord] said, Thou shalt persuade him and prevail also: go forth and do so." This passage asserts that the Lord wanted Ahab to attack Ramoth-Gilead and be killed there. Ahab himself also wanted to attack Ramoth, for he expected to capture it from the Syrians. All the false prophets, knowing the king's desire, told him what he wanted to hear and prophesied success. Jehoshaphat, however, the king of Judah, who was to accompany him in battle, wanted a prophecy from the Lord. Micaiah, a true prophet, but a man Ahab hated, was found and brought. First Micaiah agrees with the false prophets—perhaps half-heartedly or in some way disclaiming responsibility. His manner was evident, for the king said, "How many times shall I adjure thee that thou speak unto me nothing but the truth in the name of Jehovah?" Being thus put under oath Micaiah predicted death for Ahab. Micaiah even told Ahab that God had sent an evil spirit to him to entice him to his death. In spite of such plain speech, Ahab attacked Ramoth-gilead and was killed, for Ahab could not resist the lying spirit whom God sent. Ahab could not resist because God had decreed, "Thou shalt persuade him and prevail also." In the sequel God directed the flight of an unaimed arrow to the aperture in the joints of Ahab's armor, and he died. Now, note, it was as easy for God to control Ahab's decision as it was to control the unaimed arrow.

It is most probable that some persons, reading all this, will deny that the Bible says any such things; or they may, after checking in the Bible to see that the quotations made here are accurate, complain that these remarks give a very once-sided and hence distorted view of what God does.

56

The first group of people are those who think that because they are Christians (of some sort), anything they believe must be sound Christian doctrine simply because they believe it. They believe, for what reason it is hard to say, that God is not the first and ultimate cause of all things because he just cannot be the cause of evil. This point of view is of course utterly anti-Christian; the Bible contradicts it from cover to cover; and their profession of faith is no reason for supposing that their beliefs are biblical.

The second group of people are better informed. They have read the Bible and at least grudgingly admit that God is the cause of everything. But they complain that the material here covered is one-sided and therefore constitutes a distortion of the biblical position. This complaint has indeed a certain initial merit. It is true that the material of this chapter is one-sided. Whether it is therefore a distortion or not is a different question. In whatever way any book begins to explain any subject its opening argument must be one-sided, for the simple reason that all sides cannot be printed on the same page. The side that has been given in the last several pages is the side that most needs to be given. No noticeable group of people who believe in God at all denies that God causes good events, even if some deny that God causes all good events. The popular and widespread misunderstanding of the Bible consists in denying that God causes evil events. Therefore this fact must first be established by numerous examples from all parts of Scripture. This is not where the matter will be left. If the account of predestination stopped here, one could rightly say that it was not only one-sided but also distorted. The culminating and most immediate object of predestination is the salvation of believers. Faith is the gift of God, and God chooses, elects, or predestinates those to whom he will give faith. This idea, and its concomitants, will not be omitted from this explanation of predestination. And then it will be seen that the whole is not so one-sided after all. Nevertheless, in order that the happy side be properly understood and not misconceived in an unbiblical background, the present series of verses must continue a little longer. The aim is to show that God causes all things—all bad things and all good things.

The next verse is II Chronicles 25:16, which says, "Then the prophet forebare and said, I know that God hath determined to destroy thee." The prophet had just been upbraiding King Amaziah for his idolatry. The king said he had heard enough, and if the prophet did not want to be beaten up, he should keep quiet. So the prophet ended his speaking with the statement, "I know that God hath determined to destroy thee."

The next instance of God's determining and causative activity is not necessarily a causation of evil. It is a collection of events, some of which may be evil and some good. The verse is Job 14:5, which says, "His days are determined, the number of his months are with thee, thou hast appointed his bounds that he cannot pass." This verse refers to the life span of every person. "Man that is born of a woman is of few days. . . ." How long a man lives, the number of his months, is decided by God. If God has decided that Moses or Joe Doaks should live fifty-nine years, three months, and eleven days, that is it. That is the boundary or limit beyond which he cannot pass.

After Job comes Psalms, and Psalm 105:25 says, "He turned their heart to hate his people, to deal subtilly with his servants."

This is a reiteration of what was found in Exodus, and it brings us back to the title of this sub-section. The sub-section has really been aiming at two slightly different things. The main one is that God determines the choices that men make. But since men often make evil choices, some attention has also been given to the fact that God causes evil. Here the evil thing is a human choice. The Psalmist is referring to the Egyptians whom the Lord, years after the death of Joseph, caused to hate the Israelites. Hatred is a mental state, a choice, possibly an emotion. It is not merely, mainly, or even at all an overt action. It may result in overt actions, but the hatred itself is entirely mental. This mentality is what God caused in the Egyptians. God made them think that way. The verse says plainly that God turned their heart to hate his people.

Although evil and hatred have received some emphasis in this discussion, for this is what many people miss when they read the Bible, God also causes good decisions, even turning hatred to favor. For "the Lord gave the people favor in the sight of the Egyptians, so that they let them have what they asked" (Ex. 12:36). Here God completely altered and reconstructed the mental attitude of the Egyptians. Obviously he controls what people think.

The next verse contains a little puzzle that need not now be solved, for one of the points remains unaffected. Proverbs 16:1 says, "The preparations of the heart in man, and the answer of the tongue is from the Lord." The American Revised Version, the French, and German translations have it: "The plans of the heart belong to man; but the answer of the tongue is from Jehovah." At first sight the King James translation makes excellent sense, and it fits in perfectly with the course of the present argument. Thus the verse would mean that the Lord controls both what a man thinks and what he says. However, because there is a question about the translation, it would be unwise to select one that is alternative simply because it fits the present argument so well. The present argument is so abundantly buttressed that it does not need a doubtful support. The other translation might seem to say that regardless of what a man thinks on his own initiative, God controls the words he speaks; so that he may intend to deny a request for a loan, but finds himself granting it in speech. This surely cannot be what the verse means; but whatever the whole meaning may be, the idea is included that God controls what a man says.

The next verse again is not specifically a case of evil, but either good or evil as circumstances indicate. It is, however, a specific assertion that God controls men's thoughts. Proverbs 21:1 says, "The king's heart is in the hand of the Lord as the rivers of waters: he turneth it whithersoever he will." This verse states the general principle, and a particular example is found in Ezra 7:6, "And the king [of Persia] granted him [Ezra] all his request, according to the hand of the Lord his God upon him." God controls all governmental policies and decisions. Not only did God cause Pharaoh to hate the Israelites, he caused Cyrus to send the captives back to build Jerusalem. He also caused Hitler to march into Russia and he caused Johnson to escalate a war in Viet Nam. God turns the mind of a ruler in whatever direction he wants to. If now we have hesitated to say that Proverbs 16:1 asserts that God controls a man's thoughts as well as his speech, Proverbs 21:1 says so clearly. God controls the thoughts, plans, and decisions of men.

Next is Isaiah 19:17, which says, "And the land of Judah shall be a terror unto Egypt . . . because of the counsel of the Lord of hosts, which he hath determined against it." There is nothing particularly new in this verse; it is just one more that attributes to God the determination to bring trouble upon a nation.

Jeremiah 13:13-14 is similar but fuller: "Thus saith the Lord, Behold I will fill all the inhabitants of this land, even the kings that sit upon David's throne, and the priests, and the prophets, and all the inhabitants of Jerusalem with drunkenness. And I will dash them one against another." Here the destruction determined is not directed against a nation merely mentioned by name and in general, but specifically against individuals. God will fill these persons with drunkenness and dash them one against another.

To conclude this series of verses in the Old Testament, it is appropriate to quote Lamentations 3:38. "Out of the mouth of the most High proceedeth not evil and good?" Here Jeremiah confronts the objector who thinks that God sends good only and not evil. This is a fundamental misunderstanding of the divine nature and activity. God is the original cause of everything. Out of his mouth proceedeth both good and evil.

It is now time to turn to the New Testament, and once again a series of verses will be selected, beginning in Matthew and going toward the end. With the exception of the first verse they all contain the word and the idea of determination. The first verse contains the idea but not the word itself.

Matthew 26:53-54 reads, "Thinkest thou that I cannot now pray to my Father, and he shall presently [immediately] give me more than twelve legions of angels? But how then shall the scriptures be fulfilled, that thus it must be?"

"Thus it must be" are the important words. Jesus had just been betrayed. Peter, so we learn from John, drew his sword and cut off the ear of a servant. Then Jesus rebuked Peter and told him that he, Jesus, could summon twelve legions of angels; but if he did so, how could the Scriptures be fulfilled which said, thus it must be. The word *thus* includes the betrayal by Judas, the arrest, and by implication the trials, and the crucifixion. These things had to be as they occurred.

One should think carefully about the implications of prophecy with reference to the extent of God's causative activity. It is not the act prophesied that alone in its individuality is fixed and determined by God's decree. All the details that preceded the event and made it both possible

61

and actual had to be included, for otherwise the event would not have happened. Judas was chosen for his reprehensible role, but in anticipation Judas' parents had to be chosen. Does anyone think that God could have chosen Judas and could have prophesied that *thus* it *must* be, without knowing who Judas' parents were to be? If *thus* it *must* be, then it was determined that the high priest should employ a certain man as a servant and send him out that night. The man could not have fallen sick in the afternoon and taken to bed, for it *must* be *thus*. At the same time Jesus chided the officers. Why did they come upon him at night with a traitor? Could they not have arrested him in the daytime when he was teaching openly in the temple? This of course indicates the cowardly character of the priests, but the priests were cowards and the officers came at night and "*all this* was done that the scriptures of the prophets might be fulfilled."

The next six verses all contain, at least in Greek, the word determine. They each indicate some aspect of God's determination.

Luke 22:22 says, "The Son of man goeth, as it was determined: but woe unto that man by whom he is betrayed!" This verse is Christ's prediction, while still seated at the table in the upper room, that Judas was about to betray him. To be noted is the fact that what was about to happen had been determined. It was not Judas who determined what was to happen. Judas no doubt intended to betray Christ, but he might have failed. It was not he who controlled all the circumstances. Only God can determine the future. God determined how the Son of man should go.

Similarly the next verse, Acts 2:23, says, "Him being delivered up by the determinate counsel and foreknowledge of God, ye have taken and by wicked hands have crucified and slain."

The verse is similar in thought, but more explicit. In

the preceding verse it was necessary to conclude that the determining power was God by eliminating every other possibility. Here not only is God explicitly mentioned, but there is added emphasis in the words "determinate counsel and foreknowledge." This indicates deliberate planning.

As this event, the death of Christ, was foreordained, so too every event is foreordained because God is omniscient; and no detail, not even the number of hairs on one's head, escapes his foreknowledge and deliberate counsel. Everything is a part of his plan. Of everything God says, "Thus it must be."

Perhaps the most explicit and most emphatic verse along these lines is Acts 4:28. Acts 4:27-28 reads, "For of a truth against thy holy child Jesus, whom thou hast anointed, both Herod, and Pontius Pilate, with the Gentiles, and the people of Israel, were gathered together, For to do whatsoever thy hand and thy counsel determined before to be done."

Note the amount of particular detail in this passage. The context of the two verses is a spontaneous prayer on the part of a company of believers to whom Peter and John reported their experience with the Sadducees. The people thank God for the deliverance of the Apostles. They glorify God as creator. They acknowledge that he spoke through David concerning the enmity of the heathen against God. And they particularize this enmity in the recent crucifixion of Christ. "Of a truth," they say in their prayer, "in this city" (a phrase omitted in the King James version), "against thy holy servant Jesus" (servant, rather than child, in reference to Isaiah 42:1, 43:10, 52:13, and similar verses), "whom thou hast anointed" and set apart for a specific purpose, "Herod and Pontius Pilate came together with the Gentiles and the people of Israel to do whatever thy hand and thy counsel foreordained to happen." Here it says in the one word "whatever" that God foreordained or predetermined the crucifixion of Christ with all its attendant circumstances. Explicitly mentioned circumstances were the two men, Herod and Pontius Pilate. One cannot suppose that God from all eternity foreordained the crucifixion to happen on a certain date—the fulness of time, not when his hour had not yet come (John 7:30, 8:20), but only when his hour had come (John 13:1, 17:1)—and then hoped that someone would turn up to crucify Christ. Quite the contrary, Herod and Pontius Pilate were individually included in the eternal plan; and because they were so foreordained they came together to do whatever God had before decided. The word is "foreordained" or "predetermined." Must not they who say that God does not foreordain evil acts now hang their heads in shame? The idea that a man can decide what he will do, as Pilate decided what to do with Jesus, without that decision's being eternally controlled and determined by God makes nonsense of the whole Bible.

Verses enough have now been cited, but to make the array more massive a few verses of lesser importance will be added.

Acts 10:42 gives another instance of God's determining decision. The verse says, "It is he [Jesus] which was ordained of God to be the Judge of quick and dead." No comment is needed.

The next verse is Acts 17:24-26, which says, "God . . . hath determined the times before appointed and the bounds of their habitation.'" One is more impressed by the force of this verse, if one has studied the wanderings of peoples. Most high school students know of the invasions from Asia which swept over Europe around the seventh and eighth centuries. They may also remember the barbarian invasions during which Rome was sacked in A.D. 410. Later the Normans invaded France, and the Angles invaded England. It is also said that the inhabitants of France or Gaul emigrated to Galatia. And why is it that Lithuanian peasants can understand simple sentences in Sanscrit? Though it may take careful scholarship and long research to trace the paths of these migrations and to fix their dates, the cause of them all, in date, in geographical limit, and in the human decisions that initiated these movements, is the decree of God. It is God who decided which peoples should move, when they should move, and precisely where they should choose to stop moving.

Let these verses suffice for the moment.

Chapter Four

PRE-DESTINATION

With the exception of Acts 4:28 the verses quoted thus far did not use the word predestine or foreordain. The idea may have been clearly implied, but the word itself was absent. Now just a few verses must be given which explicitly use the word "predetermine" or "predestinate." Furthermore these verses provide the opportunity to show that God controls, causes, or predetermines good events as well as evil events. The latter had to be emphasized in the last chapter because the idea is shocking to many people who profess to be Christians, but who are woefully ignorant of the Bible. At the same time many of these same people deny God controls all good. Their notion of God is bizarre. If they admit that God is omniscient, and some of them deny even this, they still hold that many good events occur quite independently of God.

1. SALVATION IS OF THE LORD

The most important class of good events that God does not control are, say these people, the events of faith, acceptance of Christ, regeneration, conversion. The salvation of men, say these people, is beyond God's control. To show how anti-Christian these sentiments are, several verses will be quoted that contain the word predestinate, and then other verses will be given on the same subject, even though they do not contain that word itself.

The first passage is Romans 8:28-30, which reads, "And

we know that all things work together for good to them that love God, to them who are the called according to his purpose. For whom he did foreknow, he also did predestinate to be conformed to the image of his Son, that he might be the firstborn among many brethren. Moreover whom he did predestinate, them he also called: and whom he called, them he also justified: and whom he justified, them he also glorified."

The passage begins with the universal proposition that all things work together. That is to say, every detail of history, whether in Babylonia, Egypt, or the United States, fits into a comprehensive design. Nothing can be omitted: all things work together. Rather clearly it is God who works them together. True, the verse does not explicitly say that God works all things, but in the context of the Bible the meaning cannot be that all things are independent of divine control and through dead mechanism fit together for the purpose next stated. If "all things" were the controlling force, a complete atheism would be asserted, for the phrase "all things" is the Greek term meaning the universe. If the universe controls its details, there is no room for God.

In the theistic or biblical sense, therefore, all things conspire for the good of those who love God. It would be remarkable, would it not, if a naturalistic universe mechanically conspired for the good of a certain group of people. But this all-inclusive design is not absurd when God is in control and determines every detail for the good of those whom he has chosen, of those whom he has elected, of those whom he has called according to his deliberate purpose. God chose certain people on purpose and he works every detail of the universe for their good. The ostensible tragedy of Christ's crucifixion was intended for their good. Nero, the papacy, Napoleon, and Stalin conspire to benefit the elect. And even the fall of a sparrow. God determines everything.

Inasmuch as the last chapter said so much about God's causing evil events, it is worthwhile to point out now that these evil events are for the good of the saints. God causes evil. God also causes good. And God causes the evil as a means of blessing his people.

The verse now gives a general explanation of God's design. Whom God foreknew, he predestinated. In the discussion of Isaiah 46:10 it was pointed out that foreknowledge is not a matter of looking into the future and discovering what is there. God knows the future because he has determined it. Furthermore, foreknowledge in its biblical usage refers more to good events than to evil events. This is not to deny God's omniscience nor even his universal control. It refers merely to literary usage. Psalm 1:6 makes the contrast that God knows the way of the righteous, but the way of the wicked shall perish. Then too there is Amos 3:2, "You only have I known of all the families of the earth." Here the verb to know means to choose or select. Obviously it is not a denial of omniscience.

Therefore those people whom God foreknew, chose, or selected are precisely the individuals whom he predestinated. The Greek verb can equally well be translated predestinate or predetermine. The direct purpose of this predestination is now mentioned. God chose these people to be conformed to the image of his Son. This was of course for their good, but it was also a part of Christ's glory, for it made him the firstborn among many brethren.

Predestination is of course an act of God in eternity. That its design should be accomplished in time God called precisely those people whom he had predetermined to be conformed to the image of Christ. This calling is not the preaching of the gospel, though it occurs in conjunction with that preaching. Evangelists give a call, an external call; but God gives an internal and irresistible call. For this reason precisely the same individuals who were chosen are now called and justified. In the future these are the people whom God will glorify. It is the same group of people all the way through. No one is lost along the way; naturally not, for God works all things for their good. If God be for us, who can be against us?

The next verse in the New Testament that contains the verb predetermine is I Corinthians 2:7, which says, "We speak the wisdom of God in a mystery, even the hidden wisdom, which God ordained [predetermined] before the world unto our glory." This verse, unlike the previous passage, reflects only indirectly on God's predestination of particular persons. However, even the indirectness may perhaps have a point. Paul had preached the wisdom of God to the Corinthians. The contents of this preaching were secrets or mysteries that God had kept hidden from the Gentiles, and even from the Jews insofar as the Old Testament was not so clear as the New. This hidden wisdom had been ordained of God before the world, to confer glory on us. The accomplishment of this intention explicitly required the preaching of Paul, and implicitly his conversion, and every other circumstance that brought him to Corinth. God's predetermination therefore is universal.

But two much more important verses are Ephesians 1:5, 11. With some of the context they say, "He hath chosen us in him before the foundation of the world . . . having predestinated us . . . according to the good pleasure of his will. . . . In whom also we have obtained an inheritance, being predestinated according to the purpose of him who worketh all things after the counsel of his own will."

There are some ideas expressed in these verses that need not be discussed because, although they have their own importance, they are irrelevant to, or at least unnecessary for, the main point: for example, the idea of an inheritance, which the RSV carelessly omits from verse eleven. Nor need it be decided whether we should be blameless in love

69

or whether God predestinated us in love. These details cannot obscure the scope of predestination.

Verse four clearly teaches that before the foundation of the world God chose Paul and certain citizens of Ephesus, and by implication all the saints, for adoption. Before Cain and Abel were born, God had chosen Abel and not Cain. Before their birth God had chosen Jacob and had rejected Esau. It was certain from all eternity that Abel and Jacob would be saved and that Cain and Esau would be lost.

The means of salvation were chosen along with the persons. These persons were chosen in Christ. They were not to be saved in some other name. There is no other name by which one can be saved; and thus their relationship to Christ was fixed and predetermined before God created the world. To say, as some pseudo-evangelist may say, that God has nothing to do with a man's accepting Christ, is a sign of ignorance of, or animosity toward, the biblical message.

Verse five continues to the effect that God chose us because he had predestinated us to adoption. Greek grammar allows the participle, *having predestinated* us, to be pictured as contemporaneous with the calling, or as preceding the calling. This makes very little difference in the present discussion. The whole transaction took place in eternity before the foundation of the world. As two parts of the divine decree, it is better to call them co-eternal rather than contemporaneous. At any rate, God determined to adopt Paul and his Ephesian converts long before any of them had been born.

What is more important than the precise tense of a Greek participle is the idea that God called and predestinated us "according to the good pleasure of his will." He did not call us according to our intelligence in recognizing a spiritual blessing when we saw one. He did not choose the Jews because they were more numerous than or superior

70

to other nations. He chose whomever he chose just because he wanted to: the good pleasure of his will.

2. GOD'S GOOD PLEASURE

At this point, even at the cost of breaking the Ephesian passage in two, it seems appropriate to open a rather long parenthesis on the idea of God's good pleasure. Apparently the word occurs nine times in the New Testament. Let us see how it is used.

The Greek word is *Eudokia*. It is not a word of classical Greek, nor even of the common Greek before the time of Christ. It seems to have been used for the first time, perhaps coined for the very purpose, in the Greek translation of the Old Testament called the Septuagint. Here it translates the Hebrew word *Ratson*, a word found fifty-six times. In sixteen of these instances it refers to the will of a man, sometimes in a bad sense, such as arrogance, caprice, despotic power; for example in Genesis 49:6 it is translated self-will." Esther 1:8 has the word in a rather neutral sense. Esther 9:5 says, "Thus the Jews smote all their enemies . . . and did *what they would* [their pleasure] unto those that hated them." A distinctly good sense of the word is found in Proverbs 14:35, "The king's *favor* is toward a wise servant." Similarly, Proverbs 16:15 and 19:12.

In the Septuagint this Hebrew word *Ratson* is translated, not only by *Eudokia*, the word for "good pleasure" found in Ephesians, but also by other words meaning "will," "an act of will," and the verb "to will."

The following are some of the forty cases in which the Hebrew word refers to the pleasure or will of God: Proverbs 11:1, 20; 12:22, and 15:8 say that a just weight, righteous actions, and the prayer of the upright are a *delight* to God. The word is translated *pleasure* in I Chronicles 16:10; 29:17; Ezra 10:11; Psalm 103:21; 147:10, 11; 149:4; Haggai 1:8. I Chronicles 16:10 reads there, "Glory in his holy name, and

71

let the heart rejoice that seeks his good pleasure." The other verses say that God has pleasure in uprightness; that we should do his pleasure (twice); that God takes no pleasure in the legs of a man; but he takes pleasure in his people; that he takes pleasure in his house, or in its being built. In two verses the word is translated *will* (Deut. 33:16; Psalm 40:8). The first refers to the good will of him that dwelt in the bush [the burning bush], and the second says, "I delight to do thy will, O my God."

In the New Testament there are only two cases where *Eudokia* refers to man's will or desire. Romans 10:1 says, "Brethren, my heart's desire and prayer to God for Israel is that they might be saved." Philippians 1:15 speaks of Christian preachers who preach Christ sincerely and with a good will. All other instances refer to the good pleasure of God. To these important passages we now turn.

Chronologically the first occurrence was at the birth of Christ, when the angels sang "Glory to God in the highest, and on earth peace, good will toward men" (Luke 2:14). This verse has been seriously distorted by the tinsel of commercial Christmas advertising and the thoughtlessness of popular American religion. The idea seems to be that God promises peace and blessing to men of good will, in the sense that these men are favorably disposed to their fellows. The American Standard Version has an accurate translation that rules out this humanistic misinterpretation: "Glory to God in the highest, and on earth peace among men in whom he is well pleased." One might say, "Men of God's choice," or, very literally "men of God's good pleasure."

To suppose that men have good will, and that they consent to or agree to, or accept God's grace, is contrary to the Septuagint usage, and, since it makes salvation depend on a human act, it is contrary also to the New Testament in its entirety. *Eudokia* in this passage is God's sovereign will and cannot refer to man. Thus the angels' song is that

72

God has sent peace through Christ to the men whom he has chosen.

The next two instances, chronologically, are Matthew 11:26 and Luke 10:21. After the return of the seventy from their preaching mission, when they reported to Jesus that some men had accepted the message and some had not, so that it would be more tolerable for Tyre and Sidon, and even Sodom, than it would be for Bethsaida and Capernaum, Jesus offers up this prayer: "I thank thee, O Father, Lord of heaven and earth, because thou hast hid these things [the things the disciples preached] from the wise and prudent, and hast revealed them unto babes. Even so, Father, for so it seemed good in thy sight." Or, "for so it was well-pleasing in thy sight" (A.S.V.). Here the choice depends wholly on God's sovereign will. God hides himself from some; he reveals himself to others; and no external influence controls his choice. It is a sovereign divine decree.

The next instance of Eudokia is in Philippians 2:13, where Paul tells us to work out our own salvation. If this command seems strange to us because we are so conscious that salvation is of grace, we must remember that justification issues in sanctification, and sanctification is a process of mortifying the inclinations of the flesh and striving after personal righteousness. All this is something we do, with much effort, as John Bunyan described so well in *Pilgrim's Progress*. Nonetheless it is all by grace, for as we work out our own salvation it is God who works in us. God's work here consists of two parts: he enables us to do good deeds, but first he enables us to will those deeds; and both of these divine workings are of his good pleasure, as he sees fit, but his sovereign decree.

Now, the last instance of the word Eudokia in the New Testament occurs in II Thessalonians 1:11. It is not a very astonishing verse. Paul is simply praying that God will fulfil in us all the good pleasure of his goodness. The

73

American Revision makes it sound like a prayer that God would fulfil every desire of ours for goodness. This is an incongruous idea. The verse speaks of God's counting us worthy of his calling. The emphasis falls on God's actions, not man's; so that the next phrase must refer to God's good pleasure, not to human desires.

These are all the instances of Eudokia, except those in Ephesians 1:5 and 9. Here then the long parenthesis comes to a close, and the discussion of Ephesians resumes.

Verse 5, as was seen, says that God predestinated his saints according to the good pleasure of his will. This took place in eternity. Now in time God has made known to us the mystery or secret of his will according to his Eudokia; and to emphasize God's sovereignty the Word adds, his Eudokia which he previously set before himself as his aim or purpose. Then going on to verse 11 the Apostle says that in Christ we obtained an inheritance because we had been foreordained, predetermined, or predestinated; and this divine action occurred according to the purpose of him who works all things according to the counsel or advice of his own will. Notice that there is no external influence that turns God one way or another. As Isaiah 40:13-15 says, "Who hath directed the Spirit of the Lord? . . . With whom took he counsel and who instructed him? . . . Behold the nations are as a drop of a bucket and are counted as the small dust of the balance."

It is most appropriate to conclude this discussion of Ephesians 1:4-11 by repeating a thought from the last chapter on the eternal decree. The thought is that God controls all things. Even in this chapter we saw in Romans 8 that all things work together. This is no atheistic assertion of independent laws of a materialistic universe. It is God who works all things. Now, in Ephesians 1:11 this idea is stated explicitly. God works all things after the counsel of his own will. He does just as he pleases, with everything.

Nothing whatever escapes his predetermination.

These then are all the verses in which the word *predetermine* occurs. They are not all in which the idea occurs.
So, we proceed.

3. ROMANS IX

Many passages that do not contain the word *predetermine*
nonetheless expound the idea. The most forceful is no doubt
the ninth chapter of Romans. Let us follow through its most
important sections.

In this major epistle Paul has been explaining the doctrine of justification by faith apart from works. Two objections can be raised against this emphasis on faith apart
from the law. The first objection is that reliance on faith
and the consequent disparagement of works is an incentive
to sin. Paul answers this objection in Romans 6, 7, and 8.
The second objection is that justification by faith, the inclusion of the Gentiles, the abandonment of the Mosaic
ritual, and the condemnation of the Jews are all contrary to
the inviolable promises that God made to his chosen nation.
This second objection is answered in Romans 9, 10, and 11,
and the answer covers God's plan of world history. Here
Paul explains what God intended, how history fulfils the
prophecies, and the divine sovereignty that makes the plan
a success.

The first thing that should be said about Romans 9 is
that no interpetation of it can be correct, if it conflicts with
Romans 8. Conversely a sound interpretation is so little in
danger of conflicting that it is easy to see that Romans 9
enforces Romans 8. Paul had introduced predestination as
a basis for assurance of salvation: whom he did foreknow,
he also did predestinate, and them he also called, justified,
and will glorify. Once in the course of a conversation I re-
marked that predestination is the basis of our assurance of
salvation. The gentleman with whom I was talking and who

had been showing some aversion to the sovereignty of God exploded at this point. Why should I put such emphasis on hair-splitting, controversial doctrines! No wonder I wandered so far away from the simple Bible message! Any Christian knows that salvation is based on the shed blood of Christ, and not on some queer doctrine of predestination. Well, my friend was half-right. Our salvation from sin and hell was purchased by Christ's redeeming blood. Nothing in this book denies or conflicts with the doctrine of Christ's substitutionary death, the vicarious atonement, the *Satisfactio* of the Father's justice. But my good friend had failed to note that I was not talking about salvation per se. I was talking about our assurance of salvation. And without predestination, and the perseverance of the saints, there can be no assurance. So much for the connection between Romans 8 and Romans 9. Now for the latter chapter.

Paul begins by stating his desire that his kinsmen, the Jews, might be saved; for to them belong the adoption, the glory, the covenants, the law, the service of God, and the promises. They had a glorious heritage, but now it seems that all this had been in vain: the promises were unfulfilled and the Jews were lost. Does not this reflect on the trustworthiness of God?

The beginning of the answer is found in verse six: the word of God has not come to nought. Here one should remember Isaiah 55:11, "My word shall not return unto me void, but it shall accomplish that which I please and it shall prosper in the thing whereto I sent it." Consider this verse carefully. It says that the preaching of the gospel produces precisely the effect that God intended it should. Neither the Scripture nor even the preaching of a humble obscure minister of the Word ever fails to accomplish what God pleases. The word is sent out for a certain purpose and it prospers in that precise thing for which it was sent.

Now, we would be tempted to think that God had failed if

76

we thought God had intended to save all the Jews. Many Jews believed that no son of Abraham could be lost. But what they did not understand is that God had not chosen all. Verse six explains quite clearly that not all the citizens of national Israel are members of spiritual Israel. Nor, as verse seven continues, does physical descent from Abraham make one a child of Abraham. Abraham had two sons; but only Isaac was called. In fact, Abraham himself is an example of this restrictive divine choice, for he was called while the other citizens of Ur were not. Verse eleven continues with the most conspicuous example of divine choice and rejection. The verse reads, "For the children being not yet born, neither having done any good or evil, that the purpose of God according to election might stand, not of works but of him that calleth; It was said unto her, The elder shall serve the younger (v. 12). As it is written, Jacob have I loved but Esau have I hated" (v. 13).

The disobedience of Ishmael and Esau, occurring of course after God had rejected them, and likewise the disobedience of the Jews of Christ's day, cannot be an evidence of God's failure. This is the way God planned it. God's word does not return unto him void; it accomplishes the purpose to which it was sent; therefore God never intended to convert Ishmael, Esau, or the Jews of Christ's day. Chapter eleven shows more fully what God intended to accomplish by the disobedience of the Jews; but first chapter nine must be still further examined.

That God's plan has not failed, even when large populations reject Christ, is a very comforting thought in eras of spiritual declension. Christianity was so triumphant from A.D. 30 to 450. Persecutions, yes; troubles aplenty; heresies, a great many; but visible uninterrupted progress for four hundred years.

Then came a collapse that lasted eleven hundred years. First the invasion of the barbarians destroyed civilization and initiated anarchy. When after four centuries of anarchy, some sort of social stability had come about, the church emerged as thoroughly corrupt. There was some spiritual life among the Waldensians; Wycliffe's movement showed great promise until he died; but on the whole it was a time of incredible depravity.

Then in the sixteenth century came the world's greatest revival. For one hundred and fifty years Europe enjoyed pure Christian preaching. But the time since has been a time of deterioration, checked temporarily by limited revivals. Today we are lower than for many a century and we seem headed for the depths of spiritual ignorance and apathy. Small groups, like the Waldensians, the Wycliffites, the Hussites, will keep the gospel alive; but who can see the least ray of hope for any world-wide revival?

Has God's plan failed? No, for prophecy speaks of a coming great apostasy. This too is God's plan.

Remember, God is omnipotent. He can do anything. In fact he does whatever he pleases. Omnipotence cannot fail. Remember also that all things, even apostasy, work together for good to them whom God has chosen. Romans 8 gave us all the assurance we needed.

Paul's argument therefore, in reply to the Jewish objection, is that justification by faith does not annul the promises to Israel because the promises were not made to all the nation of Israel; they were made to the spiritual Israel of chosen individuals, the "Israel of God," as Galatians 6:16 calls them.

The next idea in the verses quoted has to do with the nature of God's choice. God's choice was an unconditioned choice. It anteceded the birth of Esau and Jacob. That the choice occurred before their birth is further emphasized by the added phrase, "neither having done any good or evil." Or, to recall Ephesians 1:4, "He hath chosen us in him before the foundation of the world." But the verse in

Romans not only emphasizes the fact that God's choice precedes our birth, it also shows clearly that God's choice does not depend on our actions or character. The twins had not done anything good or evil. The reason is that instead of God's choosing his people because they are good, they become good because he chose them. To refer again to Ephesians 1:4, Good chose us "that we should be holy and without blame."

All this is so clear that it is ludicrous how some theologians who do not like predestination try to squirm out of it. Emil Brunner attempts to convince us that Paul is not speaking about Esau and Jacob back in the times of the patriarchs. According to Brunner Paul is talking about the Edomites in the time of Malachi. Because these Edomites had done so much evil, God rejected them.

How in the world could anyone suggest such a perverse interpretation: not Esau, but Edom; not 2000 B.C., but 400 B.C.; not before doing any good or evil, but because of having done evil! To offer such a ludicrously false interpretation one has to be either the brilliant Emil Brunner or completely non compos mentis.

The reason for God's hating Esau and loving Jacob, before they had done any good or evil, is stated in verse eleven to be "that the purpose of God according to election might stand, not of works, but of him that calleth." The effectiveness of God's call is entirely because of God's power. Therefore it stands. If it depended on us, it would not stand; it would fail to accomplish its purpose. But because it is a matter of election, of divine choice, of him that calleth, and not a matter of human works, either good or evil, God's promise and purpose stands. Nothing can prevent its fulfillment. This makes it a matter of grace. Grace, omnipotence, and our assurance are ideas that fit together. If our salvation depended on our own works it would not be grace, but wages; not mercy, but justice; not sure, but impossible.

Yet this is what some ancient Jews and some modern ministers call "unrighteousness with God." In answer to this accusation Paul stresses the sovereignty of God by quoting Exodus 33:19, "I will have mercy on whom I will have mercy," and draws the immediate conclusion, "So then it is not of him that willeth, nor of him that runneth, but of God that showeth mercy." Human work and human will are set aside, for salvation is of the Lord.

Now, there are two sides to this coin, and it is impossible to have one without the other. God chose and called Abraham, but he did not choose and call the other citizens of Ur. God chose Isaac, but not Ishmael. God loved Jacob, but hated Esau. God delivered the Israelites from slavery, but he hardened Pharaoh. Some people like to dwell on the first half of the contrasts, and not only dwell on them, but even deny the second half. But the Bible gives both sides. God elects some, some only, and not others. The others were no worse than the some. In fact, the choice was made before they were born. And even after they were born, Abraham was as much an idolater as the people in Ur. There is no difference, for all have sinned and come short of the glory of God.

People who are not well grounded in the Bible take umbrage at the idea that God actually hardened Pharaoh's heart. Now, it is interesting to note that Pharaoh did not complain that God had hardened his heart. Pharaoh was quite satisfied. But others complain for him. They say God is unjust if he hardens anyone's heart. If God is omnipotent and sovereign, then it is impossible to resist his will; and if a man cannot resist God's will, why does God yet find fault?

Paul answers this objection by an appeal to the Old Testament. In Isaiah 29:16; 45:9; and 64:8 the prophet uses the illustration of the potter and his clay. The first reference says, "Shall the work say of him that made it, he made me not?" The second reference says, "Shall the clay say to him that fashioneth it, What makest thou?" And the third reference says, "We are the clay and thou art the potter, and we all are the work of thy hand." Jeremiah too, in 18:6, says, "O house of Israel, cannot I do with you as this potter? saith the Lord. Behold, as the clay is in the potter's hand, so are ye in my hand, O house of Israel." This comparison of the Lord with a potter and a man with the clay is not just a chance literary analogy. It is based on the fact that God created man and formed his body out of clay. The idea occurs twice in Job. "Remember, I beseech thee, that thou has made me as the clay" (10:9); and "I also am formed out of the clay" (33:6). Just because creation was discussed three chapters and many pages ago, it is not to be forgotten. That God makes man as a potter makes a bowl out of clay is not an illustration—it is a fact. Taking this fact and this comparison from these passages, Paul answers the objection against God's sovereign disposal of all human beings by saying, "Nay but, O man, who art thou that repliest against God. Shall the thing formed say to him that formed it, why hast thou made me thus? Hath not the potter power over the clay, of the same lump to make one vessel to honor and another to dishonor?"

Since God is the creator he cannot be unjust. He creates whatever objects, things, or persons he pleases. If he had wanted elephants with two legs and robins with four legs, he would have created them so. Created as they are, they have no ground for complaint. To understand the Bible one must realize that God is the sovereign creator. There is no law superior to him that commands, thou shalt not create elephants with two legs, or thou shalt not hate Esau. There are many details in the doctrine of predestination, and each should be given its due weight; but the basic, the final, the ultimate answer to all objections is the relative positions of Creator and creature. All objections presuppose that man is in some way or other independent of God and has obtained from somewhere or achieved by his own efforts some rights over against him. Obviously such a view is totally destructive of Christianity.

The people who object to predestination have an exalted opinion of themselves and a low opinion of God. Job, who no doubt had a more accurate opinion than these people, still had something to learn. For this reason Elihu stresses God's sovereignty and says, "God is greater than man . . . he giveth not account of any of his matters" (33:12-13). And the Lord himself adds, "Where was thou when I laid the foundation of the earth? Declare, if thou hast understanding. . . . Hast thou commanded the morning since thy days, and caused the dayspring to know his place? . . . Canst thou bind the sweet influences of the Pleiades or loose the bands of Orion?" (38:4, 12, 31). "Then Job answered the Lord and said, Behold I am vile; what shall I answer thee?" (40:4). And finally, in the American Revised Version, "I know that thou canst do all things, and that no purpose of thine can be restrained" (42:2). Job had learned his lesson.

But many modern men continue to object that this destroys free will, degrades man, abolishes morality, and makes man a puppet.

Well, it may destroy free will. Paul in Romans 9 had just said, "It is not of him that willeth." People who rely on free will must reject mercy. This is precisely the antithesis that Paul had just made. But this view does not degrade man or elephant below their proper stations, unless one thinks it is degrading to be a creature instead of the Creator. Nor does predestination abolish morality, if we pay any attention to Romans 6 and 12. Nor does foreordination or predeterminism make man a puppet.

A puppet is a jointed doll worked by strings. It operates mechanically. But Christianity neither teaches nor implies a mechanistic view of life. In Puritan times the Reformed writers constantly attacked the mechanism of Thomas Hobbes. John Gill, a great Baptist Puritan, defended Calvinism against such an objection and declared that man is "free not only from a necessity of coaction or force, but also from a physical necessity of nature." [1] In modern language this means that life is not a physico-chemical product, nor are human actions explicable by the laws of physics. The actions of puppets are.

But this is not to say that men are more independent of God than puppets are of their puppeteers. Quite the reverse. The puppeteer who wants to give a Punch and Judy show is limited in the number of things he can make his puppets do. They are jointed and controlled by strings. Therefore they cannot bend where they have no joints, nor in directions opposite to the joints' construction. Some of the charm of a puppet lies in the fact that the puppeteer can do so much even under his rigid limitations. No, man is not a puppet in God's hands. He is a lump of clay. As such the clay has no joints. Out of the same lump God can fashion a man for honor and another man for dishonor. In fact the illustration of the lump of clay does not do justice to God's sovereign control, for the human potter does not create the clay, but God does. One is not a mature or consistent Christian until with the understanding he can sing,

> Have thine own way, Lord, have thine own way;
> Hold o'er my being absolute sway.

Applying this principle to God's rejection of the Jews Paul exclaims, "What if God, willing to show his wrath and to make his power known, endured with much longsuffering the vessels of wrath fitted to destruction: and that he might

[1] *The Cause of God and Truth* (Sovereign Grace reprint), p. 188, col. 1.

make known the riches of his glory on the vessels of mercy, which he had afore prepared unto glory, even us, whom he hath called, not of the Jews only, but also of the Gentiles." The meaning of the passage is quite clear: God wanted to show his wrath and display his power. This was previously said with respect to Pharaoh: "even for this same purpose have I raised thee up, that I might show my power in thee." There are also further purposes. In the time of Paul God blinded and stupefied the Jews (Rom. 11:7-8), he cut off their branch from the good olive tree of salvation, in order to graft into that olive tree the wild Gentiles. And God will graft back again the natural Jewish branch. All this is predetermined and inevitable. It stands because of sovereign election.

Predestination therefore neither conflicts with justification by faith nor annuls the promises. These were not made to the Jews as a nation, but to chosen individuals, to Jacob, not to Esau. No, predestination does not annul the promises: it makes their fulfillment inevitable. The method by which the promises are fulfilled, not the spectacular promises of a wholesale conversion of the Jews or other world-shaking events, but the method by which the promises of salvation are fulfilled in ordinary affairs, in your life and mine, such things as regeneration and conversion, will further illustrate and explain the doctrine of predestination. To such matters we now turn.

Chapter Five

REGENERATION

The last chapter explained a number of verses that contained the idea of predestination, even though they did not contain the word itself. There is now another collection of verses, in which once again the idea without the word predestination occurs. The subject matter is closely related to predestination, and because it is a crucial point it regularly occurs in such discussions as these. People often are willing to admit that God predestined David to be king and Jeremiah to be frustrated; but what about salvation itself? Is it not up to the man himself whether or not he shall be saved? Must he not decide on his own? Must he not accept Christ for himself, of his own free will, and must not God await his decision? Now, the question of free will will be studied in the next chapter; but here is the place for considering regeneration and repentance.

As an athlete must back off a good distance to get a running start for a high jump, so too we must start further back than some people anticipate in order to surmount the problem of regeneration. In fact we must go back to eternity, before the world began. In that eternity God the Father gave a certain group of people to God the Son. Nothing much about regeneration can be understood without keeping in mind this original divine gift.

1. GOD'S GIFT TO HIS SON

The Apostle John, though he is not the only biblical author who mentions the subject, has more to say about it than any one of the others. More exactly, it is not the Apostle John, but Jesus himself who gives us the information. Read the verses carefully.

"All that the Father giveth me shall come to me. . . . And this is the Father's will . . . that of all which he hath given me I should lose nothing" (John 6:37, 39).

"Neither shall any man pluck them out of my hand. My Father, which gave them me, is greater than all" (John 10:27-28).

But the most extensive passage is Jesus' high priestly prayer in John 17. ". . . thou hast given |thy Son| power over all flesh, that he should give eternal life to as many as thou hast given him. . . I have manifested thy name unto the men which thou gavest me. . . . thine they were and thou gavest them me. . . . whatever thou hast given me are of thee. . . . I pray not for the world, but for them which thou hast given me. . . . Holy Father, keep through thy own name those whom thou hast given me. . . . those that thou gavest me I have kept. . . . Father, I will that they also, whom thou hast given me, be with me where I am."

These verses should be enough to convince everyone that God the Father gave his Son a certain number of people. But John is not the only biblical author who says so. The angel in Matthew 1:21 is not quite so explicit as Jesus was in his prayer, but nonethelsss he said to Joseph, "Thou shalt call his name Jesus, for he shall save his people from their sins." Note: *his* people.

A little less clearly Psalm 22, which anticipates the crucifixion, in verse 30 says, "A seed shall serve him." The implication is somewhat more clear in Isaiah 53:10, "He shall see his seed." These two verses by themselves do not say that God the Father gave a seed to his suffering Servant; but they do say that the Messiah has a seed or posterity, and if so, who else but God could have given it to him? The same idea is embedded in II Timothy 2:19, "The Lord knoweth them that are his." Another sidelight on the point is found in Revelation 13:8 and 21:27. In both of these verses it is said that the Lamb has a book in which are written the names of the saved, and in which other names are not written. To these verses should be added those references which speak of the sheep, e.g., John 10:3, "He calleth his own sheep by name." "His own sheep" are mentioned again in the next verse. To be sure, this is a parable, but the obvious application is that certain people are Jesus' own. Now we are back to John again, and while supporting passages may be found scattered through all the Scriptures, John speaks most clearly.

He also speaks most clearly, or at least with equal clarity, in identifying these people as the elect. Isaiah, of course, says that he shall see his seed and be satisfied. Matthew says he shall save his people from their sins; and this is clear enough. But read again the verses quoted from John and their contexts: "All that the Father giveth me shall come to me" and of all these I shall not lose even one. No one can pluck them out of my hand, much less out of my Father's hand. Again, he shall give eternal life to as many as the Father has given him. And, "Father, I will that they also, whom thou hast given me, be with me where I am."

In these verses we have the scene in eternity past and in eternity future. Before the foundation of the world the Father gave his Son a people. At the consummation and forever these people will be with Christ. But in between, in history, during our lifetime, the intermediate link of regeneration and repentance occurs. It is particularly of this that the foregoing was a preparation.

2. THE SINFULNESS OF SIN

There is also one other intervening link. Regeneration

and repentance presuppose that man is a sinner. To understand regeneration it is necessary first to understand what the sinful condition of man is. The reason for describing the condition of sinful man is to show the necessity of regeneration. Salvation must begin with a new birth. But it is God alone who chooses whom he will regenerate. Therefore because of the sinful condition of man regeneration presupposes predestination. Once again the biblical material is abundant.

It would be possible to start with Genesis 2:17, but perhaps Genesis 6:5 is more pointed: "God saw that . . . every imagination of the thoughts of [man's] heart was only evil continually." Neither Eliphaz the Temanite nor Bildad the Shuhite were prophets of the Lord; yet they spoke the truth in Job 15:14 and 25:4 where they say. "What is man . . . born of a woman, that he should be righteous. . . . How then can man be justified with God?" Though God later condemns Job's false friends, they spoke the truth on this occasion, because David in Psalm 51:5 says the same thing in stronger language. "Behold I was shapen in iniquity and in sin did my mother conceive me." Note that this was not Bathsheba who conceived a baby in sin. The reference is to David and to David's mother, and by implication everyone else. Sometime later, Jeremiah 17:9 says, "The heart is deceitful above measure and desperately wicked." In Ezekiel 37 he recounts the vision of the valley of dry bones. God asks Ezekiel, Can these bones live? Implied in God's answer to his own question is the assumption that the bones of themselves cannot produce life. Halfway through the chapter the vision changes slightly, or at least there is an addition to it. Besides the dry bones scattered around in the open valley, there were dead people in their graves. These too had no power to resurrect themselves. Only God could resurrect them and only God could choose whom to resurrect.

The Old Testament has a great deal to say about sin. The Apostle Paul in Romans chapter three summarizes a number of passages chiefly from the Psalms: "There is none righteous, no, not one; there is none that understandeth, there is none that seeketh after God. . . ." This idea, taken from Psalm 14, asserts that sin is universal (excepting Jesus only); everyone is in the same condition; they were all as dead as dry bones. These two verses also say explicitly that no one seeks after God. No doubt there is a verse that commands us, Seek ye the Lord; but the trouble is that no one obeys this command. Men ought to seek God, but no one does in his sinful condition. To put it quite plainly, no unregenerate person ever wants to be born again. For, as the Apostle goes on to say, "There is none that doeth good, no not one"; and would you not suppose that seeking the Lord in obedience to his command is doing something good? But the Apostle says no one does any good. Therefore no one seeks the Lord or wishes to be born again. Quite the contrary, "their throat is an open sepulchre . . . the poison of asps is under their lips; whose mouth is full of cursing and bitterness. . . . There is no fear of God before their eyes."

Keep in mind why Paul quotes this Old Testament material. In chapter one he showed that the Gentiles were sinners, great, gross sinners. In chapter two he showed that the Jews were worse sinners. Perhaps the Jews were not always so gross, though sometimes they had been; but aside from that, the Jews bore a greater responsibility and a greater guilt because they had received God's explicit revelation. So, the Jews, too, are sinners. Then Paul in the third chapter, grouping together Gentiles and Jews, concludes that all are sinners. The section quoted summarizes the two chapters so that "every mouth may be stopped and all the world may become guilty before God . . . for all have sinned and come short of the glory of God."

Although this passage is condensed and strong, it is not all by far. Explaining his doctrine of sanctification Paul again points out the nature of the sinful condition. In chapter eight he says that "the carnal mind is enmity against God; for it is not subject to the law of God, neither indeed can be. So then they that are in the flesh cannot please God." Consider these words carefully. Man is not merely neutral as between God and Satan. Man in his unregenerate state is positively at enmity with God. His mind is not subject to the law of God. In fact, his mind cannot be so subject. It is totally impossible for a man to obey God; in particular it is impossible for him to obey the commands, seek, repent, and believe. Man is God's enemy.

The reason unregenerate man cannot possibly seek God or repent of his sins is that he is dead, and a dead man cannot do anything. Ezekiel was not the only biblical writer who pictured sinful man as a collection of dry bones. Paul in Ephesians 2:1, 5 and Colossians 2:13 tells these people that they had been resurrected to newness of life. Dead, of course, means spiritually dead and unable to do anything to please God. The idea of resurrection obviously presupposes such a state of death. Resurrection also presupposes someone who can bring the dead to life, for quite clearly a dead man cannot raise himself. Not so pointedly and yet unmistakably Romans 6:13 says the same thing, by referring to Christians "as those that are alive from the dead."

There was a Bible teacher who told his naive, trustful students that man was sick in sin. Man was so sick that he could not cure himself. But though so sick, he could walk to the drug store and buy the medicine that would cure him. This Bible teacher did not know the Bible; he did not want to know it; for the Bible pictures man as dead, not merely as sick, and the remedy is not just a continuation and improvement of our present spiritual life, but a resurrection from the dead—a new life completely.

In the Gospels too, John 5:24-25 uses the same idea: "He that heareth my word . . . is passed from death to life. . . . The hour . . . now is when the dead shall hear the voice of the Son of God, and they that hear shall live." These verses definitely refer to the unregenerate as dead. Someone may, however, grasp at a straw and exclaim, See, the dead can do something—they can hear! Well, hardly. Lazarus was in his grave, and Christ called out, "Lazarus, come forth." Lazarus came forth all right; but it was Christ who resurrected him, gave him life, caused him to hear and live. Note that 5:25 says, they that hear, shall live. This necessarily implies that those who do not live cannot have heard. The verse therefore does not assert an ability on the part of all the dead to hear. Jesus himself said, "Ye cannot hear my word" (John 8:43). This is man's natural limitation. Only those dead hear who shall live. And only those dead hear and live who are addressed. No one else in the cemetery in which Lazarus was buried arose. The verse therefore, to repeat, does not attribute any ability to the dead in general. Lazarus alone was called.

Still someone may insist that the verse says that the dead first hear and afterward they come to life. Thus the dead, at least some dead, can do something, and if these dead can hear, then no matter who it is that is dead, his deadness does not imply that he cannot hear. To answer this ingenious argument we must read the verse a little more carefully. In fact, since the objection appeals to the tenses of the verbs, it will be necessary to study the verse's grammatical construction. If grammar is a little tedious, at least the explanation will not be very long.

The verse says the hour is coming when the dead shall hear. The future tense is used here because although the hour now is, or now is about to be, still this hour stretches out to Christ's second advent, and hence is mainly future.

91

This by itself causes no trouble. Later on some dead shall hear. But then does not the verse say that those who hear now, in the present, shall in the future, after they hear, live; and does this not imply that they hear before they are alive? No, this is not what the verse says or implies. The verse says, "The dead shall hear [future tense] . . . and the hearing-ones shall live." The KJ words "they that hear" translate a participial substantive, i.e., the participle is used as a noun. It means "the hearing-ones." Even if this past (aorist) participle functioned as a verb, as participles usually do, still it would not necessarily indicate a time antecedent to the main verb. Aorist participles may refer to earlier time, but they also refer to the same time as the main verb.[1] This participle, however, does not function as a verb, but as a noun, and the time element is virtually non-existent. If an attempt is made to preserve the time (aorist) element, the best that can be done is to take the aorist as a momentary act in contrast with the verb "shall live," that looks on into the future.

Perhaps the details of Greek grammar are hard to follow. Then all the more it is dangerous to base an argument on the ambiguous time reference of Greek participles in order to make the Apostle John contradict all the rest of the Bible and himself as well. For in a minute we shall see what else he has to say. But to conclude the explanation of John 5:25,

[1] On Greek participles, see Ernest DeWitt Burton, *Syntax of the Moods and Tenses*, page 65, §142: "The Aorist Participle is sometimes used of an action antecedent to the time of speaking but subsequent to that of the principal verb." Burton's second example is exceptionally clear, except that his qualification "antecedent to the time of speaking" plays no syntactical role. The example is Acts 25:13, "Agrippa the King and Bernice came down to Caesarea and saluted Festus." The aorist participle is "saluted" and obviously happened after the two had arrived in Caesarea. After some other examples Burton comments, "In all these cases it is scarcely possible to doubt that the participle . . . refers to an action subsequent in fact and thought to that of the verb which it follows" (p. 66).

one should realize that the meaning of the words controls the sense of the tenses. After all, a dead man, so long as he is dead, cannot hear. Hearing is a function of life. In fact, this is how the present passage began. In verse 24 John says, "The one who hears my words . . . has passed from death to life"—has already passed from death to life. Hearing in the present tense is the evidence that the one who was dead became alive in the perfect tense and so remains alive forever. Would the Apostle then in verse 25 have contradicted what he had just said in verse 24?

Other passages of Scripture also indicate that spiritual hearing and reception of the word is the effect of God's action. Isaiah 50:4-5 says, "The Lord God . . . wakeneth my ear to hear. . . . The Lord God hath opened my ear." Ezekiel 37:4 says, "O ye dry bones, hear the word of the Lord." The dry bones indeed heard, but not because of any ability inherent in dry bones. They heard because the Lord caused the breath and life, flesh and sinews, to come upon them. Jesus himself in John 8:43 asserts the inability of the Pharisees to hear his word: "Ye cannot hear my word." And very plainly, just four verses later, Jesus says, "He that is of God heareth God's words: ye therefore [note the *therefore*] hear them not, because ye are not of God." See also John 10:3, 16, 27. Would that the Arminians, who are never sure of their eternal salvation, might hear these words!

3. A NEW LIFE

That the sinful condition of the unregenerate is as described above becomes even more clear when it is explained how this sinful condition is overcome and removed. The idea of hearing Christ's word, the idea of a spiritual resurrection, the idea of God's gracious act of regeneration, all enforce the previous description. The next paragraphs therefore, beginning with some verses from John again,

93

will discuss irresistible grace, regeneration, faith, and repentance.

What the Bible says about regeneration, spiritual resurrection, or the new birth confirms everything already said about predestination. The first passage to be examined is John 1:12-13. When John wrote his Gospel toward the end of the first century, many people had accepted Christ. These are the many who received him. "To them gave he power to become the sons of God . . . which were born, not of blood [Greek: bloods], nor of the will of the flesh, nor of the will of man, but of God." Interest attaches to the method of regeneration. Verse 13 does not first say how regeneration is accomplished; it first tells how regeneration is not accomplished. The people referred to were not born again "by blood" (more accurately, by bloods). The Jews of Christ's day generally believed that physical descent from Abraham guaranteed their salvation. John the Baptist rebuked them: "Think not to say within yourselves, we have Abraham to our father" (Matt. 3:9). And Paul declares that "they which are of faith, the same are the children of Abraham" (Gal. 3:7). Blood or race therefore is not the cause of regeneration. The second and third ways not to be born again are the will of the flesh and the will of man, or, better, the will of a man.

The distinction between the second and the third points, the will of the flesh and the will of a man is probably that the will of the flesh refers to human nature in general. All men by birth are estranged from God. There is nothing in general human nature that would lead a man to eternal life. This has already been amply explained by the description of man's sinful condition. The third point contrasts general human nature with one, any one, man. A given man might think that regardless of the condition of other men, and regardless even of his own sinful state, he can decide on his own to accept Christ and be saved. This is

94

what John denies. No one is born again by an act of his own will. No one can possibly misunderstand the text. It says quite flatly that those who receive Christ were born, not by the will of a man, but by God.

To become Christian a person must be born again, born into God's family. We all were "children of wrath, even as others" (Eph. 2:3), and we had to be reborn as children of God. Obviously this is something a man cannot do. When one is "born of the Spirit" (John 3:6), it is the work of the Spirit. A baby cannot initiate its birth. This is the act of its parents. No baby chooses or decides to be born. This is why the spiritual change from the death of sin to newness of life is pictured as a birth. The picture of resurrection teaches the same lesson. We are raised from the dead; but we do not raise ourselves, it is the act of God. Hence the will of man has nothing to do with this in the least. Arminian dependence on the human will simply makes salvation impossible. Some Arminians may have indeed been saved—by blessed inconsistency. But Arminian preaching, such as that of the evangelist Charles G. Finney, is an unmitigated tragedy. Earlier as John Wesley sank deeper and deeper into his semi-romish, anti-biblical persuasion, George Whitefield wrote a letter of condemnation. It would prove instructive if contemporary Christians, who by and large have never learned the lessons of the Reformation, would read and consider carefully the warnings of the saintly George Whitefield.

4. WHITEFIELD AND HUTCHESON

Whitefield had learned that John Wesley was about to publish a sermon on predestination. On June 25, 1739, he wrote privately to Wesley and urged him not to publish it. On July 2, 1739, he wrote again: "Dear, honored sir, if you have any regard for the peace of the church, keep in your sermon on predestination." As soon as Whitefield left England in August 1739, Wesley published his sermon, entitled *Free Grace*, and attached to it a hymn by his brother Charles on *Universal Redemption*. Between August 1739 and early 1741, Whitefield wrote several times to Wesley, trying to persuade him to return to the biblical teaching. In one letter he said, "What a fond conceit it is to cry up *perfection* and yet cry down the doctrine of *final perseverance*. But this and many other absurdities you will run into because you will not own *election*. . . . O that you would study the covenant of grace." In 1741 Whitefield made public his letter of December 24, 1740. It is a long letter of eighteen printed pages (in the Banner of Truth edition of *Whitefield's Journals*, 1960).

Following are some excerpts from this letter. "Honoured sir, how could it enter into your heart to chuse a text to disprove the doctrine of election out of the eighth of Romans, where this doctrine is so plainly asserted that once talking with a Quaker upon the subject, he had no other way of evading the force of the Apostle's assertion than by saying, 'I believe Paul was in the wrong.' . . . Had you written clearly, you should first, honoured Sir, have proved your proposition 'that God's grace is free to all . . . but you knew that people . . . were generally prejudiced against the doctrine of *reprobation* and therefore thought that if you kept up their dislike of that you could overthrow the doctrine of election entirely. . . . I frankly acknowledge I believe the doctrine of reprobation.

. . . This is the established doctrine of Scripture, and acknowledged as such in the seventeenth article of the church of England, as Bishop Burnet himself confesses; yet dear Mr. Wesley absolutely denies it."

The long letter should be read in its entirety, but since this is not the place to go too deeply into eighteenth century history, we shall return again to the first century and John's Gospel.

John's Gospel contains other supporting verses. They are so clear that it is difficult to explain how Wesley and Finney could have failed to see them. "The wind bloweth where it listeth . . . so is everyone that is born of the Spirit" (John 3:8). If contemporary Christians are not familiar with the work of Whitefield, they are even less conversant with the Puritans, great and small. George Hutcheson was perhaps midway between great and small. One of his comments on John 3:8 will add an historical as well as an exegetical note to the discussion. In his *Exposition of the Gospel according to John* he says at this place, "The Spirit's working is compared to wind, not only here, and in that extraordinary pouring out of the Spirit, Acts 2:1-2, but Canticles [Song of Solomon] 4:16; not only because the Spirit and wind have one name in the original languages of the scriptures, but because of many things wherein the one resembleth the other; and in the text . . . we have these: 1. As the wind bloweth through the world freely, not staying for the command, nor caring for the prohibition, of any creature, so the Spirit, in his working, is a free agent, working where, on whom, when, and in what measure he pleaseth, and will be hindered by none. . . ."

That no one can hinder divine causality John asserts again in 5:21, "As the Father raiseth up the dead and quickeneth them [makes them live], so the Son quickeneth whom he will." Here again is the figure of a resurrection, rather than a rebirth. But the concepts are the same. It is a matter of producing life. Who is to be reborn or resurrected depends totally on the will of God. The Son quickens whom he will. No one can stay his hand; no one can resist his will. The matter lies entirely in God's hands. God is irresistible.

5. IRRESISTIBLE GRACE

Sufficient emphasis has now been given to the significance of rebirth and resurrection as figures of speech for the action of God's Holy Spirit. Now under the notion of irresistible grace the Bible continues to reveal the causative power of predestination in the lives of dead sinners.

The Bible speaks many, many times about irresistible grace. In addition to the previous anticipatory verse, consider the following list.

Ezekiel 11:19 says, "And I will give them one heart, and I will put a new spirit within you; and I will take the stony heart out of their flesh, and will give them an heart of flesh." This verse says that God will do something. He will remove a stony heart and transplant a heart of flesh and put a new spirit in the patient. This patient did not ask for a transplant. His stony heart was quite satisfied with itself. It was at enmity with God. It would have resisted the operation, if it could have done so; but it could not. God's power is irresistible; and if God says, I will remove your heart and give you another, he will do it, and none can stay his hand. The same thing is repeated almost verbatim in Ezekiel 36:26-27.

Without this divine act the man's condition is hopeless. Preaching produces no saving effect. The sinner is unable to believe. John 12:38-39 quotes Isaiah 53:1 and adds the implication, "Therefore they could not believe," after which he makes another quotation from Isaiah. That salvation rests on divine initiative and not on the will of man is indicated again in John 15:16, "Ye have not chosen me, but I have chosen you." This verse does not explicitly state that Christ's choice is irresistible, but the preceding verses have said so, and the . .lowing will say so again.

Acts 13:48 asserts that "as many as were ordained to eternal life believed." If they could have resisted this ordination, they would not have believed. Since they all without exception believed, they must have been irresistibly foreordained. Further on in Acts 26:18 there is a description of Paul's conversion and its motivation. The motive was God's. God determined to send Paul to open the eyes of the Gentiles and to turn them from the power of Satan unto God that they might receive forgiveness of sins. Now, it would seem that this verse presupposes that God can defeat Satan and convert the Gentiles. But the more obvious reference to irresistible grace lies in Paul himself. God determined to use Paul. He intended to make him a minister and a witness, and eventually to stand before King Agrippa, as here in this chapter. Could God have failed? Could Paul have resisted? Could a creature defeat the plan and intention of the Creator? God had created Paul for this purpose. It is ridiculous to suppose that the lump of clay, this time formed into a vessel of honor, could have resisted the divine Potter.

Read II Corinthians 4:6, "God hath shined in our hearts to give the light of knowledge of the glory of God in the face of Jesus Christ." Could God shine and we prevent light? If he puts knowledge in our minds, can we decide to be ignorant?

Why is it that a man, a dead sinner, turns to God? The answer to this question was known to the Old Testament saints. David in Psalm 65:4 states, "Blessed is the man whom thou choosest [Paul, for example], and causest to approach unto thee." Like Adam upon his fall, like Cain after the murder of Abel, like the wicked kings of Israel, sinners do not want to approach God. They want to flee from him, put him out of their minds, and worship creeping things or golden calves rather than seek God's face. This would they all do, this would we all do, unless God chooses some and causes these people to approach his holy temple.

Ephesians 2:5 and Philippians 2:13 have been already discussed, so we may now turn to I Thessalonians 5:9, "God hath not appointed us to wrath, but to obtain salvation by our Lord Jesus Christ. And II Thessalonians 2:13-14, "God hath from the beginning chosen you to salvation . . . whereunto he called you . . . to the obtaining of the glory of our Lord Jesus Christ." Salvation was the purpose of God's appointment and for this purpose he chose us. How could anyone resist and nullify what God did "from the beginning"? Now, finally, for this series of verses, James 1:18 reads, "Of his own will begat he us with the word of truth." This reinforces John 1:13. We were begotten by God's will. Can a child not yet begotten prevent the begetter from begetting him? A plain question like this shows what nonsense is involved in denying irresistible grace and predestination.

6. ARMINIANISM

This is as appropriate a place as any to sketch the Arminian theology that so directly attacks these pervasive elements of the biblical revelation. This theology, introduced into Protestantism by James Arminius (Jacob Hermandszoon), whose doctrines were condemned by the Synod of Dort in 1620, but which lived on in John Wesley and Charles G. Finney, holds that God elects persons to eternal life, not of his mere good pleasure as the Bible says, but on condition of their voluntary reception of grace and their perseverance therein. This makes God's decree depend on man's independent choice and ability to lead a Christian life.

In the next place these people hold that Christ's death does not save anyone. Christ did not intend to save anyone. He had neither Abraham nor Paul in mind. He did not die for definite individuals; he did not love *me* and give his life for *me*, as Paul says in Galatians 2:20; but he died for all men indiscriminately. In so dying for all men en masse, he rendered salvation merely possible to all men indifferently, but he did not make salvation actual for anyone. He did not really save anybody. For on this Arminian view Christ on the cross was not a substitute for Peter, James, John, and the elect. He did not pay the penalty for me. He did not intend to save any particular person.

In making salvation actual for some men the Holy Spirit, on the Arminian view, exercises the same influence on all men universally. There is no work of irresistible grace. The Spirit treats all men alike. Some are saved because they cooperate with him. Others are lost because they resist him. Actual salvation depends on the will of man rather than the will of God.

On this scheme salvation is not made certain by Christ's sacrifice. In fact, salvation is not certain at all. A man who at one time cooperates with the Spirit and truly believes may later be lost. No one can have assurance in this life that he will arrive in heaven. There is always the possibility that the free and mutable will of man will falter and change, in which case the man will become unregenerated.

Clearly the Arminians do not have the Gospel. They have no good news. They leave man in uncertainty and despair.

7. FAITH

This short discussion of Arminianism shows well enough the importance of the *application* of redemption. God's eternal decree is not the whole story; nor is Christ's death on the cross. The effects of these must terminate on individual sinners. One effect is regeneration. This has already been discussed. Irresistible grace is another factor in the application of redemption. Now, the next factor in the application of redemption to the individual sinner is faith, saving faith in Jesus Christ.

An evangelist, a faithless evangelist, told a group of people who came forward at his invitation that God could not cause them to accept Christ, but that if by their own will they decided for Christ, then God would regenerate them. I assure the world, as the inspired Psalmist authoritatively did so long ago, that God can and does *cause* sinners to seek his face. I can also assure the world, as Paul more authoritatively did, that no one was ever saved by this type of "evangelism." It is not evangelism because it is not the evangel. It is not the Gospel. It is not good news. It is a scheme of salvation by human will power. But a dead man cannot seek God; he cannot exercise faith in Jesus Christ. Faith is an activity of spiritual life, and without the life there can be no activity. Furthermore, faith is not the result of man's so-called free will. Man, all by himself, cannot produce faith. It does not come by any independent decision. The Scripture is explicit, plain, and unmistakable: "For by grace are ye saved through faith, and that not of yourselves, it is the gift of God" (Eph. 2:8). Look at the words again, "It is the gift of God." If God does not give a man faith, no amount of will power and decision can manufacture it for him.

At a certain graduation ceremony I heard a seminary president misinterpret this verse. His misinterpretation did not succeed in ridding the verse of the idea that faith is the gift of God, though that was presumably his intention. He based his argument on the fact that the word *faith* in Greek is feminine, and the word *that* in the phrase, "and that not of yourselves," is neuter. Therefore, he concluded, the word *that* cannot have *faith* as its antecedent. The antecedent, according to this seminary president, must be the whole preceding phrase: "For by grace are ye saved through faith." Now, even if this were correct, faith is still a part of the preceding phrase and is therefore a part of the gift.

Taking the whole phrase as antecedent makes poor sense. To explain that grace is a gift is tautologous. Of course if we are saved by grace, it must be a gift. No one could miss that point. But Paul adds, "saved by grace, through faith," and to make sure he also adds, and *that*, i.e., faith, is not of yourselves.

But what of the president's remark that *faith* is feminine and *that* is neuter. Well, of course, these are the genders of the two words; but the president did not know much Greek grammar. In the case of concrete nouns, e.g., the mother, the ship, the way, the house, the relative pronoun that follows is ordinarily feminine; but what the president did not know is that abstract nouns like faith, hope, and charity use the neuter of the relative pronoun. As a matter of fact, even a feminine thing, a concrete noun, may take a neuter relative (cf. Goodwin's *Greek Grammar* § 1022). The moral of this little story confirms the original Presbyterian policy of insisting upon an educated ministry. Here was a seminary president distorting the divine message because of ignorance of Greek[1]—or, more profoundly, as I have reason to believe from some of his publications, because of a dislike for divine sovereignty.

To return now from these grammatical remarks to the sense of the verse itself, one can easily see that a giver chooses whom he will to give something to; and if he does not choose a particular person, that person does not get the gift. The gift in this case is a certain mental activity, called believing; in concrete, believing in Christ. It is not just any kind of faith, for although the verse itself does not explicitly say faith in Christ, no one can rationally deny

---

[1] A. T. Robertson in his *A Grammar of the Greek New Testament*, p. 704, lists six exceptions to the common rule that adjectives agree in gender with their nouns: Acts 8:10, Jude 12, II Peter 2:17, I Peter 2:19 ff., I Cor. 6:11, and 10:6. These include masculine pronouns with feminine nouns, neuter adjectives with feminine nouns, and neuter adjectives with masculine nouns. The most interesting in the present connection is I Peter 2:19, where twice there is a neuter demonstrative with a feminine noun, thus paralleling Eph. 2:8. I dutifully report that Robertson strangely asserts that the neuter demonstrative in Eph. 2:8 does not refer to the noun faith. He gives neither a grammatical nor a theological reason for this assertion.

103

that the context implies that Christ is the object of that faith. Note well, God does not give his chosen recipient a general mental ability to believe. General mental ability was a gift to all humanity in creation. This mental ability has been vitiated by sin, and mankind is guilty of wrong thinking. But for this very reason, it is not so much the mental ability per se that is harmed by sin (though in another connection this is true and pertinent also) as it is the voluntary choice of objects to believe. The most blatant sinner can very well believe in social security or the United Nations. But he cannot believe in Christ. Faith in Christ is a gift, a gift obviously given to some men only, and not to all. These "some" are the ones God has chosen, elected, or predestinated.

Parenthetically one may here note that attempts to improve on the King James version are not always commendable. *The New English Bible* reads, "For it is by his grace you are saved, through trusting him; it is not your own doing. It is God's gift, not a reward for work done. There is nothing for anyone to boast of." Although this is not the worst possible translation, it does not maintain the level of accuracy required for Bible translation. It says, "by his grace" and this means Christ's grace; but the actual text does not indicate whether it is Christ's grace or the Father's. It simply says, "by grace"; why not leave it that way? Second, it does not make the possible correction in the next phrase: "by grace you have been saved." So, here there is no improvement over King James. Third, the N.E.B. says, "through trusting him," instead of "by faith." Above it was pointed out that by implication the object of faith is Christ; but it is implication and not explicit wording. A good translation must follow the words and not insert the implications. Then for a final point, although the N.E.B. uses the word "work" and says "not a reward for work done," the omission of the word "faith" results in a weakening of the contrast between faith and works. This weakening is further seen in that the N.E.B. does not make it clear that the gift God gives is faith.

Although the verse in Ephesians is the best known verse that declares faith to be a gift, there are others. Romans 12:3 also says that faith is a gift and adds that God decides the size, extent, or measure of the gift. The words are, "think soberly, according as God hath dealt to every man the measure of faith." The context makes it clear that "every man" does not mean every man in the whole world, but "every man that is among you" Roman Christians. To these persons God has measured out different "amounts" of faith. Some men believe more, some believe less. How much a man believes no doubt depends immediately on how much he understands. As Paul had said in the tenth chapter, a man cannot believe unless he has heard the good news. But ultimately how much of the good news he believes depends upon God's measuring it out to him. This is a far cry from the fundamentalistic evangelist's insistence that the unregenerate will, God standing aside and helpless, can produce faith of itself. Whether a man believes anything, and how much he believes is determined by God.

Ephesians 6:23 implies the same thing, when Paul in his benediction says, "Peace . . . and love with faith from God the Father." Philippians 1:29 enforces the idea: "Unto you it is given . . . not only to believe on him, but to suffer for his sake." The main idea here is to prepare the Philippians for persecution, but a part of the preparation is the knowledge that God gives them faith.

Less explicit, because it is a description of the results of evangelistic efforts, but nonetheless quite obvious, is Acts 11:21. When the disciples were scattered abroad because of persecution, they preached the Gospel wherever they went, "and the hand of the Lord was with them, and a great number believed." The heathen believed, of course, because the hand of the Lord was with the Christians and made their preaching effective. Also less explicit, but still far removed from the notion of faith as a totally human possibility for unregenerate men, is I Corinthians 2:5, which says, "That your faith should not stand in the wisdom of men, but in the power of God."

More explicit again is I Corinthians 12:9: "For to one is given by the Spirit the word of wisdom, to another the word of knowledge by the same Spirit, to another faith by the same Spirit." The list of the Spirit's gifts continues and includes miracles, prophecy, and tongues. Note that faith is as much a gift as the power to work miracles; and who would claim that unregenerate man (unless possessed by Satan) could of himself perform miracles?

These verses are perhaps the most important verses that declare faith to be the gift of God. The Scriptures contain a multitude more, describing the nature of faith, the results of faith, and personal examples of faith. None of these passages deny that faith is a gift from God, and if they do not explicitly say that God produces faith, their contexts imply or presuppose it.

8. REPENTANCE

After faith, the next factor that must be discussed in the application of redemption to the individual is repentance.

The first thing to be done here is to understand the meaning of the word repentance. The word itself is rather unfortunate. It was introduced into the English language and the KJ version under the influence of Jerome's Vulgate translation of the Greek text. Jerome's Latin was better than any other translation of his day, but among his faults was his use of *penance* instead of what we now call repentance. To do penance is to attempt to pay the debt for sin.

106

No one other than Christ can do this; and to confuse *Metanoia* with doing penance has resulted in a good deal of evil. The Greek word in the New Testament is *Metanoia*. Unfortunately it is too late to change the English language; but we must be careful to see what precisely the New Testament means.

The best definition I know of repentance is that of the Shorter Catechism: "Repentance unto life is a saving grace, whereby a sinner, out of a true sense of his sin, and apprehension of the mercy of God in Christ, doth, with grief and hatred of his sin, turn from it unto God, with full purpose of it, and endeavour after, new obedience."

First of all, it is to be noted that the topic is repentance unto life. This is a species of a genus that includes other types of repentance. The New Testament word *Metanoia* means a change of mind. But of course men change their minds on all sorts of subjects. Under the control of certain ideas, a father may intend to give his young son a sled for Christmas; but then he changes his mind, accepts other ideas, and decides to give him an electric train. This is an instance of *Metanoia*, repentance, a change of mind; but of course it is not the particular change of mind the New Testament talks about.

Repentance unto life is indeed a change of mind. Previous ideas are set aside, new beliefs are accepted, and as a result different conduct ensues. The new ideas, to which the sinner changes, are summarized in the Catechism. Previously he had incorrect ideas about sin; he changes to a true concept of sin. Previously he had wrong ideas about God. Now he has a true apprehension of the mercy of God in Christ. To be sure, and especially in this twentieth century, he may have thought that God was merciful, so merciful that he would never punish anyone. He probably thought also that Christ was not necessary to a satisfactory religion. But now he has a true, not a mistaken, apprehension of God's mercy, as it occurs only in Christ. Because of these new ideas, he turns with grief and hatred of his sin unto God and endeavors to obey his laws. Such is the particular change of mind that the English of the KJ version designates as repentance.

Now, the connection with predestination more directly concerns another point. The first phrase of the Catechism is, "Repentance unto life is a saving grace." When one sees not only that this is what the Catechism says, but that the Catechism correctly summarizes the Bible, one will see more clearly how repentance and predestination must go together.

If repentance is a grace, it is unmerited favor. The mental action of repentance, the substitution of Christian for secular ideas, is the favor or gift of God. When Peter preached to Cornelius, he did not quite understand how God would handle the Gentiles. He already knew that repentance was a gift from God. Then when Cornelius received the Holy Ghost, Peter and those to whom he later recounted the episode said, "Then hath God also to the Gentiles granted repentance unto life" (Acts 11:18). Repentance is a grant, a gift, given by God to the particular individuals he chooses.

God does not choose to give repentance to all men. In II Timothy 2:25 the Apostle writes, "In meekness instructing those that oppose themselves, if God peradventure will give them repentance to the acknowledging of the truth." Obviously not everybody repudiates his secular ideas and acknowledges the truth. But some do. Here the apostle tells us how to conduct ourselves in the presence of those who pursue their own destruction, for maybe God will give repentance to some of them. Naturally it is God who chooses to whom he will make this grant.

God's choice is made against a background. The whole of history fits into a unified scheme. Therefore in Acts 5:31

Luke, quoting Peter, writes, "Him hath God exalted . . . to give repentance to Israel." There can be no repentance unto life apart from Christ. But this all the more emphasizes God's control.

The same idea, albeit not the same word, occurs in the Old Testament too. Zechariah 12:10 is, "And I will pour upon the house of David, and upon the inhabitants of Jerusalem, the spirit of grace and of supplications: and they shall look upon me whom they have pierced, and they shall mourn for him, as one mourneth for his only son, and shall be in bitterness for him, as one that is in bitterness for his firstborn." Supplications and mournings are the effect of God's pouring out his Spirit on the house of David. Supplication is not the result of any natural inclination to seek God, for no one of himself seeks God, no, not one.

Not so explicit, but supporting the main idea, is II Corinthians 7:10: "Godly sorrow," i.e., sorrow *according to* God, as the Gospel *according to* John, its author—"Godly sorrow worketh repentance." The cause of the sorrow is God.

In conclusion, this chapter has shown that the application of redemption to individuals is caused by God. As for regeneration, man takes no part at all. He does nothing. God does something to him. Human will has no role at all. In the cases of faith and repentance, man indeed does something. Faith and repentance are mental activities, combining the intellect and the will. The man must understand and believe. But though these are things the man does, it is God who causes him to do them, and without this causality the man simply could not have this state of mind. Salvation is of the Lord.

Chapter Six

FREE WILL

The previous chapters have been a straightforward exposition of several hundred verses of Scripture. They have fully established the doctrines of creation, omniscience, the eternal decree, predestination, and the application of redemption. In this chapter exposition gives place to rebuttal; many people have raised objections against these doctrines, and here an answer is given to one of them. This means that there will be less exposition, for the exposition is really completed, and more argumentation. There will be enough Bible; all the previously quoted passages will be the foundation; but there will be some philosophy and a little bit of history too.

1. A LITTLE PHILOSOPHY

One of the standard objections to predestination is that it conflicts with free will. The person who makes this objection is undoubtedly correct on one thing, viz., free will and predestination are contradictory concepts. No one who knows the meanings of the terms can believe both doctrines, unless he is totally insane. But not everyone knows what the words mean.

The idea of free will, or, more vaguely freedom, is very fuzzy; or perhaps one should say the term freedom has been applied by different writers to quite different things. It strikes me that there is a wider range of meanings among the very well educated than among the ordinary populace.

Common people, whether Christian or not, seem to have a clear and accurate notion of free will; whereas philosophers differ with each other and sometimes with themselves.

For example, the seventeenth century Descartes, the founder of modern philosophy, not only diverged from the common meaning, but may have been self-inconsistent too. In his fourth *Meditation* he writes that "the faculty of will alone, or freedom of choice [is] so great that I am unable to conceive the idea of another that shall be more ample and extended; so that it is chiefly my will which leads me to discern that I bear a certain image and similitude of Deity . . . for the power of will consists only in this, that we are able to do or not to do the same thing . . . or rather that . . . we so act that we are not conscious of being determined to a particular act by any external force." The first half of this quotation seems to reflect common opinion: there are no conceivable limits to freedom. Even God's freedom is no more ample and extended than my own, he says. But the second half seems to make freedom consist in our ignorance of the external force that controls the will. Surely this is not what most people mean. Freedom must mean the absence of limitation, not the ignorance of what the actual limitations are.

On the same page Descartes says something else also that is inconsistent with the idea of absolute freedom seemingly asserted at the beginning of the quotation just made. "To the possession of freedom," he says, "it is not necessary that I be alike indifferent towards each of two contraries; but, on the contrary, the more I am inclined towards the one, whether because I clearly know that in it there is the reason of truth and goodness, or because God thus internally disposes my thought, the more freely do I choose and embrace it; and assuredly divine grace and natural knowledge, very far from diminishing liberty, rather augment and fortify it." He then goes on to say that the liberty of in-

111

difference is the lowest grade of liberty and "manifests defect or negation of knowledge rather than perfection of will."

In these words Descartes maintains that if either knowledge or divine grace controls and determines the will, we are more free than if we had the liberty of indifference. The predetermining force of grace augments and fortifies liberty. To the present writer this seems to be very close to the truth; but in any case it is inconsistent with freedom of will as this is commonly understood in objections against predestination.

If here Descartes seems to incline towards Calvinism, in *The Principles of Philosophy* I, 41 he favors the Romish and more common view. In this paragraph he asserts that God, in spite of omniscience and predestination, "leaves the free actions of men indeterminate"; and he bases this assertion neither on the Bible, nor on logical deduction, but on immediate experience. "We have such a consciousness of the liberty and indifference which exists in ourselves that there is nothing we more clearly or perfectly comprehend." This is an assertion that Spinoza later blasted to bits by pointing out that consciousness of liberty cannot be distinguished from ignorance of determination. Little Tommy, age four, stamps his foot, throws a tantrum, and wants what he wants when he wants it. He knows he is free because he does his wanting so energetically. But if his mother is wise, she knows that he is acting up because he has missed his nap. Tommy is ignorant of what causes affect him. So too are most, doubtless all, adults. But ignorance is not freedom.

Aside from Spinoza's argument, Reformation Christianity insists on appealing to Scripture, not to experience. It was Schleiermacher who introduced experience into "Christian" theology, and modernism was the outcome. No doubt all of us have experience, experiences, of many types; but the analyses of these experiences cannot be made by our ordinary human resources. Even if trained psychologists think that human resources are sufficient for discovering the causes of behavior, they would agree that people who are not trained psychologists are incompetent to make the analysis. Really the psychologists are incompetent too, for unless an analyst be omniscient, his failure to discover a cause of the action would not prove freedom. It only proves ignorance. Only omniscience could know that no cause anywhere is affecting a person's conduct. Apart from omniscience the cause may be real enough but remain undiscovered. Hence anyone who claims to know by immediate experience that he has free will, is claiming to be as omniscient as God. A Christian, however, does not analyze his experience. A Christian knows that he is neither omniscient nor infallible. Therefore he turns to the Bible to find God's analysis of his experience. This is what we propose to do.

The question therefore is, Does the Bible teach the freedom of the will? By freedom of the will is meant what most ordinary people mean: the absence of any controlling power, even God and his grace, and therefore the equal ability in any situation to choose either of two incompatible courses of action. There are some semi-calvinists who, presumably through fear, assert the freedom of the will, and then more or less disguise the fact that they define freedom of will in a way most people would never guess. In a similar situation Pascal, in his Provincial Letters, excoriates the Dominicans for using Jesuit terms with Jansenist meanings. The Jesuits were too powerful; they were about to crush the Jansenists; and the Dominicans were afraid. Pascal makes the point that Jesuit terms will convey Jesuit meanings to the populace, and hence the Dominican theology, in thought similar to Jansenism, will be defeated by the terms it uses. So too semi-calvinists who use Arminian terms support Arminianism, for the populace will never discover their esoteric definitions. Freedom of will, almost universally, means that God does not determine a man's choice. It means that the will is uncaused, not predetermined. The present book uses "free will" in its ordinary, commonly accepted sense. The question is: Does the Bible teach freedom of the will?

It is so obvious that the Bible contradicts the notion of free will that its acceptance by professing Christians can be explained only by the continuing ravages of sin blinding the minds of men. To some this sounds like an extreme statement. But the appeal is to the Bible, and the Bible says that the heart of man is deceitful above measure. It will use all possible devices to avoid acknowledging that it is a worm, a lump of clay, a creature, and not an independent, autonomous being.

The appeal is to the Bible. This appeal has been made extensively in the preceding chapters. It will be made again in this chapter. But first a little church history will be helpful.

2. MARTIN LUTHER

After the time of the Apostles the immediate need of the Church was to formulate and defend the deity of Christ, which it did in the doctrine of the Trinity in the Nicene Creed. The next thing was to maintain that Christ was one person with two natures. This was settled in the creed of Chalcedon. Then Augustine could take up the doctrines of sin, grace, and predestination. The Church up to this date had not thought much about these doctrines. Even Augustine himself in his first attempts did not quite grasp what the Bible meant. But later in life he wrote two tractates that everyone should read: *Grace and Free Will* and *Predestination*. The position there taken has characterized Augustinians or Calvinists from that day to this.

Political anarchy with its attendant suppression of learning and moral decay plagued the visible church for the next thousand years. In the ninth century one Gottshalk preached predestination, and for doing so was put in jail until he died. For several decades in the fourteenth century Wycliffe shed some biblical light in England. But the great Reformation began with Luther in 1517.

The Reformation got a good start by emphasizing grace and denouncing penance and indulgences. Grace and justification by faith alone soon led to questions of predestination and free will. One of Luther's opponents was Erasmus. Erasmus had made a name for himself by writing satires on the monks, but in a more scholarly way by collating a few Greek manuscripts and publishing, i.e., printing, a Greek New Testament for the first time. Neither of these events made Erasmus a Lutheran, however. In defense of Romanism Erasmus published a book on free will.

From a scholarly viewpoint this book was a pretty poor production. Luther thought it so poor that he paid no public attention to it. Because of his silence the rumor started that Luther had met his match, that he could not answer Erasmus, and that his movement had to fail. Luther's friends pressed him to answer Erasmus.

Luther considered this useless because so easy. But the popular rumors forced him to write a book of some 400 pages entitled *The Bondage of the Will*. In addition to Augustine's tractates everybody ought to read this book by Luther. It will be clearly seen that Protestantism began with a denial of free will, and that its reintroduction into Protestant churches a century later was a step back toward Romanism and justification by works.

When Luther was convinced that he had to write against Erasmus, he discharged his obligation with such vigor and such fulness that it makes quotation difficult. Each small point is discussed so thoroughly that few paragraphs are sufficiently complete in themselves to make good quotations. But we can try a few.

For although you think and write wrong concerning "Free-will," yet no small thanks are due unto you from me, in that you have rendered my own sentiments far more strongly confirmed, from my seeing the cause of "Free-will" handled by all the powers of such and so great talents, and so far from being bettered, left worse than it was before: which leaves an evident proof, that "Free-will" is a downright lie; and that, like the woman in the gospel, the more it is taken in hand by physicians, the worse it is made.[1]

This, therefore, is also essentially necessary and wholesome for Christians to know: that God foreknows nothing by contingency, but that He foresees, purposes, and does all things according to His immutable, eternal, and infallible will. By this thunderbolt, "Free-will" is thrown prostrate, and utterly dashed to pieces. Those, therefore, who would assert "Free-will," must either deny this thunderbolt, or pretend not to see it, or push it from them (pp. 38-39).

Upon the authority of Erasmus, then, " 'Free-will,' is a power of the human will, which can, of itself, will and not will to embrace the word and work of God, by which it is to be led to those things which are beyond its capacity and comprehension." If then, it can will and not will, it can also love and hate. And if it can love and hate, it can, to a certain degree, do the Law and believe the Gospel. For it is impossible, if you can will and not will, that you should not be able by that will to begin some kind of work, even though, from the hindering of another, you should not be able to perfect it. And therefore, as among the works of God which lead to salvation, death, the cross, and all the evils of the world are numbered, human will can will its own death and perdition. Nay, it can will all things while it can will the embracing of the word and work of God. For what is there that can be any where beneath, above, within, and

[1] Luther, Martin, *The Bondage of the Will*, p. 17. Sovereign Grace Union, 1931.

116

without the word and work of God, but God Himself? And what is there here left to grace and the Holy Spirit? This is plainly to ascribe *divinity* to "Free-will." For to will to embrace the Law and the Gospel, not to will sin, and to will death, belongs to the power of God alone: as Paul testified in more places than one (p. 127).

Not that I say this, as approving the Sophists concerning "Free-will," but because I consider them more tolerable, for they approach nearer to the truth. For though they do not say, as I do, that "Free-will" is nothing at all, yet since they say that it can of itself do nothing without grace, they militate against Erasmus, nay, they seem to militate against themselves, and to be tossed to and fro in a mere quarrel of words, being more earnest for contention than for the truth, which is just as Sophists should be. But now, let us suppose that a Sophist of no mean rank were brought before me, with whom I could speak on these things, in familiar conversation, and should ask him for his liberal and candid judgment in this way: —"If any one should tell you, that that was *free*, which of its own power could only go one way, that is, the bad way, and which could go the other way indeed, that, the right way, but not by its own power, nay, only by the help of another — could you refrain from laughing in his face, my friend?"—For in this way, I will make it appear, that a stone, or a log has "Free-will," because it can go upwards and downwards; although, by its own power, it can go only downwards, but can go upwards only by the help of another[2] (p. 130).

The sense, therefore, is this: —seeing that so many depart from the faith, there is no comfort for us but the being certain that "the foundation of God standeth sure, having this seal, The Lord knoweth them that are His. And let every one that calleth upon the name of the Lord depart from evil" (2 Tim. ii. 19). This then is the cause and efficacy of the similitude—that God knows His own! Then follows the similitude—that there are different vessels, some to honour and some to dishonour. By this it is proved at once, that the vessels do not prepare

[2] The Sophists Luther mentions are not ancient Greeks but a certain group of medieval theologians.

themselves, but that the Master prepares them. And this is what Paul means, where he saith, "Hath not the potter power over the clay," &c. (Rom. ix. 21). Thus, the similitude of Paul stands most effective: and that to prove, that there is no such thing as "Free-will" in the sight of God. (p. 264).

I here omit to bring forward those all-powerful arguments drawn from the purpose of grace, from the promise, from the force of the law, from original sin, and from the election of God; of which, there is not one that would not of itself utterly overthrow "Free-will." . . . The arguments, I say, I omit to bring forward, both because they are most manifest and most forcible, and because I have touched upon them already. For if I wished to produce all those parts of Paul which overthrow "Free-will," I could not do better, than go through with a continued commentary on the whole of his epistle, as I have done on the third and fourth chapters. On which, I have dwelt thus particularly, that I might shew all our "Free-will" friends their yawning inconsiderateness, who so read Paul in these all-clear parts, as to see any thing in them but these most powerful arguments against "Free-will;" . . . (pp. 360-361).

I shall here draw this book to a conclusion: prepared if it were necessary to pursue this Discussion still further. Though I consider that I have now abundantly satisfied the godly man, who wishes to believe the truth without making resistance. For if we believe it to be true, that God fore-knows and fore-ordains all things; that He can be neither deceived nor hindered in his Prescience and Predestination; and that nothing can take place but according to his Will, (which reason herself is compelled to confess;) then, even according to the testimony of reason herself, there can be no "Free-will" —in man, — in angel, —or in any creature! (p. 390).

Although the following reference is not to Martin Luther, it may be inserted here as a bit of church history and an evidence of what the Reformation really stood for. William Tyndale in *An Answer to Sir Thomas More's Dialogue*

(Parker Society Reprint, 1850, p. 191), writes, "Why doth God open one man's eyes and not another's? Paul forbiddeth to ask why. . . . But the popish can suffer God to have no secret, hid to himself. They have searched to come to the bottom of his bottomless wisdom; and because they cannot attain to that secret, and be too proud to let it alone, and to grant themselves ignorant . . . they go and set up free-will with the heathen philosophers, and say that a man's free will is the cause why God chooseth one and not another, contrary to all Scriptures."

3. APPEAL TO SCRIPTURE

So much for history. The substantial question is settled only by an appeal to Scripture. Of course Augustine and Luther, not to mention Calvin, appealed to Scripture. The previous chapters of this book were a massive appeal to Scripture. It might be difficult to find any more such clear and definite verses. But there is one verse, mentioned above in connection with the *Eudokia* of God, that in its other phrases is so clear that the Arminians must be terribly embarrassed by it. Before the verse is quoted, however, one more paragraph of philosophy will be inserted.

It is a sound principle to let the Bible speak for itself. Nearly every Christian agrees that one should not impose an alien philosophy on the Bible or try to understand its teaching on the basis of secular presuppositions. In my experience, however, some people who have most loudly said so have been the very ones who have most extensively violated this perfect precept. The basic reason for their procedure may very well be the noetic or mental effects of original sin; but the immediate cause is their ignorance of philosophy. Since they have never studied secular philosophy, they believe they are innocent of such false doctrine; and how then could they impose on Scripture philosophical ideas they never learned? What these people fail to notice

119

is that the philosophic ideas of great men filter down to the general populace after a century or so. What Schleiermacher in Germany said in 1800 became popular American preaching in the early twentieth century. The science, in particular the physics, of the late seventeenth century remains in the common mind today, even though ninety-nine percent of the scientists have given it up either wholly or in large part. Hence people who have not studied philosophy are the very ones who are least able to see when it is being imposed on the Bible. Thus it is, coupled with man's sinful desire to be independent of God, that people who think they are very good Christians defend freedom of the will.

Now, among the many biblical passages that deny free will, there is one so clear and so pointed that I do not see how anyone could possibly misunderstand it. In Philippians 2:12-13 the Apostle Paul tells us to "work out your own salvation with fear and trembling, for it is God which worketh in you both to will and to do of his good pleasure." The A.S.V. changes this only to make it say, "for it is God who worketh in you both to will and to work, for his good pleasure." Even the untrustworthy R.S.V. has essentially the same thing: "for God is at work in you, both to will and to work for his good pleasure." The KJ translation seems to be the best.

Now, then, what does the verse say? Well, of course, it says that we should work out our own salvation. Let us be quite clear on the fact that the Bible does not teach *salvation* by faith alone. The Bible teaches *justification* by faith alone. Justification then necessarily is followed by a process of sanctification, and this consists of works which we do. It consists of external actions initiated by internal volitions. We must therefore work out our own salvation; and this, in fear and trembling because we must depend on God. What then does God do in our process of sanctification? The verse says, God works in us. It is a very good thing that God

120

works in us, for if he did not, we would have cause for a fear and trembling of quite a different sort. God works in us—that is clear enough. But the verse is more definite and tells us two things God does in us. First, he so works in us that we do the things that produce sanctification. God works in us so that we sing a psalm, or comfort the sick, or apprehend a criminal, or preach the gospel. These are things we do because God works in us to do them. But there is something preceding this doing on which the doing depends. We would do none of these things if we did not first will to do them. Now, the verse clearly states that God not only works the *doing* in us, but he first works the *willing* in us. God works in us *both* to will and to do.

Other verses, such as Ephesians 1:11, previously quoted, said that God works *all* things universally. This verse states in particular that God works our own willing. It is clear therefore that man's will is not free, but is directed by the working of God. And to conclude with a reminder, both this verse and those that say God works all things add, "of his good pleasure." It is God's mere good pleasure, it is just because he wanted it so, it is nothing other than his sovereign decision, that we do what we do and will what we will.

In many discussions on free will, after quoting and explaining a dozen or more verses, and after having met stubborn opposition to the Reformation doctrine, I have often said, Well, then, you give me the verses on which you base your idea of free will. This challenge usually produces a blank stare. No verses are needed, they say. Everybody knows he is free. In other words, these people who have studied no philosophy are unaware that they are repeating Descartes to the effect that it is impossible even to conceive of a more ample freedom than that of the will of man, and almost quoting his very words, "We have such a consciousness of the liberty and indifference which exists in ourselves that there is nothing we more clearly or perfectly comprehend." Thus they try to impose a secular philosophy on the Bible.

A little extra emphasis can well be put on the fact that there are no verses in the Bible that assert free will. In the Old Testament several verses speak of free-will offerings. This has nothing to do with the topic of free will. In the Old Testament the Law required the Israelites to give tithes. Beyond this legal obligation they could of course give more. The widow's mite was far more than a tenth of her substance. This is what was called a free-will offering. Of course the term *free-will* is English. The Hebrew term means, abundantly, willingly, spontaneously, freely, voluntarily. The question as to God's determining or not determining the volition is absent from the texts. Nor is Ezra 7:13 an exception: the same word is used, and repeated in Ezra 7:16. Even if the heathen king had used the English term free will, we would not be impressed with his theology. At any rate, Artaxerxes merely means that if anyone wishes to go to Jerusalem, he may. Whether or not God inclines the Israelite to decide to go is not considered. Besides, does anyone know an Arminian who bases his theory on Ezra 7:13?

Usually Arminians naively base their theory on many biblical statements that say this man and that man willed to do this and that. Well, of course, the Bible clearly asserts that men will. But the question is not whether they will, or have a will, but whether God determines their will. The question is not whether a man chooses; but whether his choice had a cause or reason. The Calvinist does not deny will or volition; he denies that volition like all the rest of creation is independent of God.

The Calvinist may even say that will is free, not absolutely, or free from God, but free from the laws of physics and chemistry. Indeed the Calvinist reacts strongly against behaviorist determinism. But he asserts divine predetermination, foreordination, predestination.

This explains a chapter in the Westminster Confession that puzzles some people. They note that chapter nine is entitled "Of Free Will." So, does not the Confession assert free will? Not necessarily. The present chapter also is entitled "Free Will," but obviously it does not assert free will. One must read what the chapter says. Now, the Confession says, "God hath endued the will of man with that natural liberty, [so] that it is neither forced, nor by any absolute necessity of nature determined, to good or evil." Neither this paragraph nor the three Scripture references under it (one of which will be considered later on in the present chapter) have anything to say about God's relation to the will. What is asserted is that voluntary acts are not physically forced (as in behaviorism) nor determined by any absolute necessity of nature.[1]

If a student wishes to know what the Confession teaches about God's control of the will, as distinct from nature's lack of control, let him read section four of the same chapter and section one of chapter ten. Surely the Confession does not contradict itself on the same page.

Chapter IX, 4 says,

> When God converts a sinner, and translates him into the state of grace, he freeth him from his natural bondage under sin, and by his grace alone enables him freely to will and to do that which is spiritually good; yet so as that, by reason of his remaining corruption, he doth not perfectly nor only will that which is good, but doth also will that which is evil.

Still more explicit is chapter X, 1, which says

> All those whom God hath predestinated unto life, and those only, he is pleased, in his appointed and accepted

[1] Cf. *What Do Presbyterians Believe* (pp. 105ff.), by the present writer.

time, effectually to call, by his word and Spirit, out of that state of sin and death in which they are by nature, to grace and salvation by Jesus Christ; enlightening their minds spiritually and savingly to understand the things of God; taking away their heart of stone, and giving unto them an heart of flesh; renewing their wills, and by his almighty power determining them to that which is good; and effectually drawing them to Jesus Christ; yet so as they come most freely, being made willing by his grace.

Note that by his almighty power God determines the wills of men. Granted that this section is concerned only with those whom God has predestined to life, it still says that God determines human volitions. The predestined saint comes to God freely, i.e., willingly, or voluntarily, but only after God has made him willing.

To the Confession one may add Question 67 of the Larger Catechism. The wording is similar. "Effectual calling is the work of God's almighty power and grace, whereby . . . renewing and powerfully determining their wills, so that they . . . are hereby made willing. . . ," etc. An opponent of determinism will not find much comfort here.

It will not escape the keen observation of those who have turned their backs on Luther and Calvin to return, not to Paul, but to Erasmus and Rome, that so far only one verse, and not dozens, has been brought forward. This deficiency can be easily and extensively remedied. In fact it has already been done.

4. FURTHER SCRIPTURES

A previous indication that man's will is not free is the fact that no man can defeat the will of God. For example, God had foreordained David to be King of Israel; but if this be so, then not only was it impossible for Goliath to kill David and defeat God's will, but it was also impossible for David to decline the honor and refuse to be king. Goliath's inability was no doubt physical; but David's was

124

entirely psychological, mental, volitional. He could not have willed to remain a mere shepherd boy. His will was not free. He had to will to accept the Kingship. One verse that states this idea in general form is Isaiah 46:10, "My counsel shall stand and I will do all my pleasure." The following verse reiterates the idea: "Calling a ravenous bird from the east, the man that executeth my counsel [the man of my counsel] from a far country: yea, I have spoken it, I will also bring it to pass; I have purposed it, I will also do it." The man from the far country had to come because·Psalm 33:11 says the same thing: "The counsel of the Lord standeth forever." Therefore David's choice was predetermined.

To proceed on from David, these verses in Psalms and Isaiah also apply to Cyrus. Since the Lord had foreordained Cyrus to rebuild Jerusalem, Cyrus could not have willed otherwise. Consider Proverbs 21:1, which says, "The king's heart is in the hand of the Lord: he turneth it whithersoever he will." It is amazing that anyone who calls himself a Christian and has read even a little part of the Bible can deny that God controls the mental operations of his creatures. The heart of man is in the hand of the Lord and the Lord turns man's heart in any direction the Lord pleases. The idea that man's will is free, independent of God, able to turn itself in any one of a dozen incompatible directions, is totally unbiblical and unchristian. As a clear denial of omnipotence, it dethrones God and takes man out of God's control.

Sometimes people try to avoid these conclusions by asserting that God is indeed omnipotent, that he can control everything, but that he has abdicated and has left men free. Now, in the first place, if God can control man's will, then even if he abdicates control, man's will is not the per se autonomous, inviolable personality that these people also say it is. But what is more important, even if some Arminians escape this inconsistency, the assertion that

125

God can but does not exercise control is, by the Bible, false. The Bible repeatedly asserts, not that God can but does not, but that God does exercise this control. This is what Psalm 105:25 says: "He turned their heart to hate his people." The whole Psalm is a list of things that God not only can do, but has done. He sent Joseph into Egypt to prepare for the time of famine; later he sent Moses; he smote the first-born; he gave his people the lands of the heathen. In the middle of this recital of his wondrous works the Psalm says that God made the Egyptians hate the Israelites. If hatred were merely an emotion, the verse would still show that God controls the conscious mental activities of men. But in addition to the mere emotion, hatred presupposes an object to hate; this object must be a known object; and the hatred involves some very definite ideas concerning that object. The verse therefore teaches that God controls our ideas and thoughts. We think what we think, choose what we choose, and love or hate definite objects because God has predetermined such mental actions.

Two further Old Testament verses may be mentioned. Ezra 6:22 says, "For the Lord had made them joyful, and turned the heart of the King of Assyria unto them." Note, God not only could; he did. There is no abdication of power. Next, I Samuel 2:6-7 says, "The Lord killeth, and maketh alive: he bringeth down to the grave, and bringeth up. The Lord maketh poor and maketh rich: he bringeth low and lifteth up." He not only can; he does.

A New Testament example may now be added. Since God had predestined to introduce Cornelius and the Gentiles into the Christian church, Cornelius could not have refused, nor could Peter have willed to remain in Joppa that day. Peter was not free to will just anything. It had been pre-determined in eternity that he should will to go to Caesarea. He could not possibly have willed otherwise, for God's counsel stands, he does all his pleasure, and none can stay his

126

hand or say, What doest thou?

It is hardly worthwhile to multiply examples. Not only Cornelius but all the elect were chosen before the foundation of the world. In this connection something must be said about regeneration, repentance, and faith. The discussion of these topics, given elslewhere, can be understood to apply here. But the present chapter is more directed against an objection and for this purpose more general principles make a better answer.

Those theologians, Romanists and Arminians, who argue in favor of free will, sometimes says that God simply cannot "violate a man's personality." In fact I have run across some who speak explicitly about the sovereignty of man. Usually these people affirm that God is clever enough to outwit men and will therefore be able to control the general course of history and especially bring it to a satisfactory conclusion. But many of the details God cannot control because he has no power over man in his freedom. The illustration of a game of chess is used. The world champion, God, cannot dictate the moves of his opponent, but he can invariably check-mate him.

This is an attractive illustration, but it illustrates nothing in the Bible. Aside from everything else in the Bible two verses in Jeremiah dispose of the sovereignty of man and his immunity from divine intervention, even in the inmost recess of his will. These verses do not mention man's will. As is so often, or in fact always, the case, the verses imply more than they say. For this reason Christians usually see much less in the Bible than what is there. Unaccustomed to deducing conclusions logically they stop at the surface of the text and plunge no deeper. But the Bereans were noble precisely because they compared Scripture with Scripture and drew conclusions. In the present instance even comparison is unnecessary. The verses themselves imply the conclusion.

Jeremiah 32:17 reads, "Ah, Lord God, . . . there is nothing too hard for thee." Ten verses later the text uses a rhetorical question, "Behold, I am the Lord, . . . Is there anything too hard for me?" Come to think of it, this sentiment is a familiar one, not original with Jeremiah, for Genesis 18:14 reads, "Is anything too hard for the Lord?"

Now, what does "anything" include? Of course it includes Sarah's bearing a son at an old age. It also includes the capture of Jerusalem by the Chaldeans; for these two events are those specified in the contexts. But the principle itself is far wider. When God wanted to convince Abraham and Sarah that they would have a son, he did not say, "I can give you a son"; he said, "I can do anything." Therefore the general principle applies to anything and everything. It follows therefore that God can control the will of man. And as for the inviolability of personality, man has no "rights" that are inviolable by God. God is the creator; man is a creature. "Who art thou that repliest against God?" Just return to chapter one on the creation. Omnipotence settles the argument. Therefore God can control man's will, and the examples show that he does.

Would it be tedious to examine another example? Perhaps it would be tedious, but it would show how utterly the Bible is opposed to Arminianism, Romanism, and free will. The Bible constantly contradicts the notion that God cannot and does not control the thoughts and decisions of men. How God can fulfill prophecy and direct the course of history without determining the volitions of the agents is something the opponents of foreordination cannot explain. The Bible itself never faces this difficulty. It identifies many acts of will that God determined. II Chronicles 10:15 gives us an excellent example. Rehoboam had just succeeded his father Solomon. The people of Israel petitioned him to reduce taxes. Solomon's advisers urged Rehoboam to grant the people's request, but Rehoboam's young friends persuaded him to reject the petition and to threaten that he would chastize them with scorpions. "So the King hearkened not unto the people, for the cause was of God, that the Lord might perform his word, which he spake by the hand of Ahijah the Shilonite to Jeroboam the son of Nebat." This refers to an event described in I Kings 11:29ff. The prophet Ahijah met Jeroboam and gave him God's message that "I will rend the Kingdom out of the hand of Solomon, and will give ten tribes to thee."

This promise was kept, the prophecy was fulfilled, Jeroboam got the ten tribes of Israel; how he got them is set forth in the Chronicles passage. It occurred by God's causing the people to decide to petition the King, and by God's causing the King to accept the bad advice of the young men, and by God's causing the people to decide to rebel under the leadership of Jeroboam. The overt actions could not have occurred without the several acts of will on the part of the agents. Their decisions are an essential and indispensable part of the history. Had these people been free from divine foreordination, had God not determined them, God himself could not have been sure that the prophecy would prove true. The K.J. version says the cause was of God; the A.S.V. translates it, "it was brought about of God, that Jehovah might establish his word." It could be translated, "the turn of affairs was of God." Whatever the translation, the idea is that God not only could, but did control all the factors, and among these the decisions or volitions of men were essential.

5. ARMINIAN VERSES

Perhaps someone may think that justice has not been done to the verses Arminians often use. It is not enough to say that no verses explicitly teach free will, for maybe some teach it by implication. Therefore a number of such verses need to be studied. John Gill, a great Baptist Puritan,

129

studied 250 such verses. Here a few will be taken up. In most cases John Gill's argument will be abbreviated or even amended slightly; in two very important cases he will be quoted verbatim and in entirety. Perhaps the reader may decide to read the complete original. Its title is *The Cause of God and Truth*.

One verse used against predestination is Deuteronomy 5:29, which says, "O that there were such an heart in them that would fear me . . . that it might be well with them and with their children forever." The Arminians argue that this desire of God is inconsistent with decrees of election and reprobation. If there were such decrees, the sentiment of this verse would be hypocritical. The verse implies, say the Arminians, that God gives to all men sufficient grace for conversion, while man's acceptance or use of this grace depends on his own free will.

It is not hard to answer this Arminian argument. First, God's strong and sincere wish for the salvation of some men is entirely consistent with a decree to elect these persons. To make their point, the Arminians would have to show that God desired the salvation of all men; but this verse refers only to Israelites. If any verse seems to say that God desires the salvation of all and is not willing that any should perish, it will be discussed in its proper order. Here at least the wish is restricted to a few people. If this verse or any verse speaks of God as wishing the salvation of someone whom he has rejected as reprobate, there would be an inconsistency implying hypocrisy. But this is not the case here, for here God is speaking of his chosen people.

John Gill further argues that God's wish in this verse does not refer to salvation in heaven, but to salvation from earthly tragedies and to temporal prosperity in the promised land. Though this idea may surprise some people, the last verse of the chapter makes it plausible because it speaks of "prolong[ing] your days in the land which ye shall possess."

Nevertheless some people may suppose that this argument dodges the important question. They may say that temporal prosperity anticipates eternal salvation, just as Christ's acts of physical healing entailed forgiveness of sin. The Arminian argument would then be: God desires the salvation of all the Israelites, but some were lost. Therefore unless God is hypocritical, the doctrine of predestination and the decrees must be abandoned.

To this form of the argument it must be shown, as has already been done in the earlier chapters of this book, that God the Father gave his Son a certain people; and that he died to redeem these particular individuals and no others. Christ died for the sheep, and not for the wolves; on the cross he intended to save Abraham and Paul, but he did not intend to save the wicked men of Sodom. His intention was fulfilled because the Scripture says that he shall see his seed, his word will not return void, it will accomplish precisely what was intended, and he shall be satisfied.

As for the Israelites who were lost, Paul reminds us that they are not all Israel, which are of Israel; but that there is an Israel of God; and so all Israel shall be saved. This should do for Deuteronomy 5:29.

John Gill also studies Deuteronomy 30:19, which says, "I have set before you life and death, blessing and cursing; therefore choose life, that both thou and thy seed may live."

On this verse Gill begins, "These words are frequently made use of by the patrons of free will." He then demolishes the doctrine of free will more comprehensively than the present book has allowed itself. He points out that even the Arminians must deny free will to Satan, since admittedly he cannot will anything good. It should also be noticed that God cannot will to do anything evil; nor can the good angels; nor can the redeemed in heaven. In none of these

131

cases does the person have equal ability to will either of two incompatible lines of action. In none of these cases is there any liberty of indifference. God's will is of course "free" in that no superior beings control him; but this fact gives no support to human free will as it has been defined. Gill's five columns of rather small print explaining the functions and limitations of the will must be omitted here. So far as the verse in Deuteronomy is concerned, it is enough to repeat that Calvinists do not deny that man chooses. The question is: Does God cause the choice? The verse by itself has nothing to say, one way or the other, on the cause of choice. But for Arminian use it would have to deny such causation explicitly.

Psalm 145:9 reads, "The Lord is good to all, and his tender mercies are over all his works." The Arminians assert that this sentiment is contrary to the doctrines of election and reprobation. One writer asks, "Why is it said that his tender mercies are over all his works, if they are so restrained from his most noble creatures?" And another one writes, "It should not be said, his tender mercies are over all his works; but his cruelties are over all his works." The latter writer was a bit too enthusiastic, for clearly predestination places God's tender mercies over at least some of his works, however much his cruelty or severity is shown to others, as Romans 11:22 teaches.

Setting aside this Arminian exuberance and addressing oneself to the more sober objection, one may insist that predestination does not restrain the tender mercies of God over all his works, not even excluding the reprobate. Even people who have no share in God's special grace experience divine mercies. For there are several sorts of mercies. Not all are inseparably joined to salvation. Such mercies even the reprobate can enjoy. "God "maketh his sun to rise on the evil and on the good, and sendeth rain on the just and on the unjust" (Matt. 5:45). The more extreme Arminians anticipate the Universalists, who deny that anyone is lost: they reject the idea of hell and teach that all are saved. But as the Bible clearly teaches that not all are saved, it follows that God's mercies are of several kinds, and his special saving grace is not a necessary adjunct of other kinds. This is obvious also from another direction. The Psalm does not say merely that God's mercies are over all mankind. It says that they are over all his works. But if so, God's tender mercies are over animals, plants, and inanimate objects; and no Arminian is likely to claim that these are all objects of salvation. There are therefore several kinds of tender mercies. God bestows some of these on the reprobate. Hence the doctrine of predestination does not contradict Psalm 145:9.

In fact, the doctrines of predestination and so on represent God as being more, not less, merciful than the doctrines of conditional election and free will. Calvinism maintains that the salvation of some is certain, guaranteed, and sure. Salvation as the Arminians describe it is uncertain, precarious, and doubtful. In their view salvation depends on the mutable, independent will of man. They even hold that a man once saved can be lost, saved again, and finally lost. The Calvinists maintain that the mercy of God is such that he holds his own in his hands and that no one, not even the man himself, can pluck them out of the Father's hand.

The opponents of predestination use several biblical commands as if they were inconsistent with the Calvinistic position. An example, that can stand for other similar verses, is Isaiah 1:16, 17: "Wash you, make you clean." This command is supposed to imply that a man can wash himself clean, or not, as he chooses. The "or not" presumably supports free will, and the ability implied in the command opposes total depravity, and both together refute irresistible grace. The argument is, if conversion were wrought only by the irresistible grace of God, and man were purely passive therein, these commands to wicked men are useless and indeed hypocritical.

In answer to this Arminian argument, the first thing to insist upon is that men are filthy and need to be washed; but more than this, they are so filthy that they cannot clean themselves, either by Old Testament ceremonial ablutions or by any New Testament ordinance. Proverbs 20:9 asks the rhetorical question, "Who can say, I have made my heart clean?" The cleansing of the heart is God's work, for it is God who creates a clean heart within and washes sinners thoroughly from their iniquities (Ps. 51:2, 10). Recall also Ezekiel 36:25, "Then will I sprinkle clean water upon you, and ye shall be clean; from all your filthiness and from all your idols will I cleanse you."

At this point the nonplused Arminians reply, But if this is the work of God alone, and man does not help in it at all, then of what use are these commands? Since they must be of some use, man must be able at least to help in cleansing himself.

This reply, however, fails because it is based on a logical fallacy. It supposes that since the command cannot have the use the Arminians want it to have, it can have no use at all. Since the Scripture very clearly says that man cannot cleanse himself at all, one must see what use the Scripture assigns to such commands. This is not hard to do. Romans 3:20 says, "By the law is the knowledge of sin." Commands are given, not because any man can obey them, but in order to convince man that he is a sinner. Let him try to obey and he will find he cannot. When a man discovers this, he will be more willing to see the need of divine grace. Proverbs 30:12 mentions "a generation that are pure in their own eyes, and yet is not washed from their filthiness." The commands under discussion are intended to convince some sinners that they are not clean and that they cannot wash themselves. Hence the commands are not in vain, nor do they contradict the gospel of grace.

There is another command, which though similar in nature to the preceding gives opportunity for a further development of the argument. Jeremiah 4:4, almost a verbatim repetition of Deuteronomy 10:4, says, "Circumcise yourselves to the Lord, and take away the foreskins of your heart." These words supposedly imply that man is not totally depraved, but that he is able to save himself, and that God does not exercise irresistible grace; for, if the Calvinistic doctrines were true, the command would be useless.

The question concerning the uselessness of commands has already been answered; but note further in connection with this verse that the figurative expression of circumcising the heart very probably does not refer to regeneration or conversion. When God commanded Abraham to circumcise Isaac, Abraham was already a sincere worshiper of God. So too was Isaac. Instead of this verse having to do with regeneration, it more probably indicates some works subsequent to regeneration. It means that the people now being regenerate should immediately begin to mortify the deeds of the flesh and strive toward righteousness. This interpretation would empty the verse of all Arminian value.

However, it is possible that the verse could refer to regeneration. Even so, it has no Arminian value. We read in the New Testament about the circumcision of the heart, in the Spirit and not in the letter, whose praise is of God, not of men (Romans 2:29). Note that literal circumcision was performed by a man, and insofar as it was done in obedience to God, the man was worthy of a measure of commendation: the Lord could say, Well done, thou good and faithful servant. But this circumcision is not performed by a man. It is a circumcision made without hands (Colossians 2:11). Even circumcision of the flesh, administered to infants, expresses the passivity of the recipient. If this is

135

true of the type and Old Testament shadow, it must be much more true of the New Testament reality. Incidentally, the translation, Circumcise yourselves, could be improved to "Be ye circumcised." The verb here and in the Septuagint is passive. Even the Latin Vulgate has the passive voice.

For a final remark on this verse, note that what God here commands, Be circumcised, he elsewhere promises to do himself. Deuteronomy 30:6 says, "The Lord thy God will circumcise thine heart . . . that thou mayest live." From none of this can the Arminians derive any aid or comfort.

Other Old Testament verses which the Arminians use, or used to use in the eighteenth century, must be omitted. One of the first verses in the New Testament is a well-known verse that Arminians use today, and they have used it on the present writer several times. It is such a popular verse with them that I shall quote John Gill in full. He has five remarks to make. If some people are puzzled by his second remark, none the less the other four are clear enough.

> O Jerusalem, Jerusalem, thou that killest the prophets, and stonest them which are sent unto thee, how often would I have gathered thy children together, even as a hen gathereth her chickens under her wings, and ye would not! —Matt. 23:37.

Nothing is more common in the mouths and writings of the Arminians than this Scripture, which they are ready to produce on every occasion, against the doctrines of election and reprobation, particular redemption, and the irresistible power of God in conversion, and in favour of sufficient grace, and of the free-will and power of man, though to very little purpose, as will appear when the followings things are observed.

1. That by Jerusalem we are not to understand the city, nor all the inhabitants; but the rulers and governors of it, both civil and ecclesiastical, especially the great Sanhedrin, which was held in it, to whom best belong the descriptive characters of *killing the prophets*, and *stoning* such as were *sent* to them by God, and who were manifestly distinguished from their *children;* it being usual to call such who were heads of the people, either

136

in a civil or ecclesiastical sense, *fathers*, Acts vii. 2, and xxii. 1, and such who were subjects and disciples, *children*, xix. 44, Matt. xii. 27, Isa. viii. 16, 18. Besides, our Lord's discourse, throughout the whole context, is directed to the Scribes and Pharisees, the ecclesiastical *guides* of the people, and to whom the civil governors paid a special regard. Hence it is manifest, that they are not the same persons whom Christ would have gathered, who *would not*. It is not said, *how often would I have gathered you, and you would not*, as Dr. Whitby more than once inadvertently cites the text; nor, *he would have gathered Jerusalem, and she would not*, as the same author transcribes it in another place; nor, *he would have gathered them, thy children, and they would not*, in which form it is also sometimes expressed by him; but *I would have gathered thy children, and ye would not*, which observation alone is sufficient to destroy the argument on this passage in favour of free-will.

2. That the *gathering* here spoken of does not design a gathering of the Jews to Christ internally, by the Spirit and grace of God; but a gathering of them to him externally, by and under the ministry of the word, to hear him preach; so as that they might be brought to a conviction of and an assent unto him, as the Messiah; which, though it might have fallen short of saving faith in him, would have been sufficient to have preserved them from temporal ruin, threatened to their city and temple in the following verse—*Behold, your house is left unto you desolate*: which preservation is signified by the *hen gathering her chickens under her wings*, and shows that the text has no concern with the controversy about the manner of the operation of God's grace in conversion; for all those whom Christ would gather in this sense were gathered, notwithstanding all the opposition made by the rulers of the people.

3. That the will of Christ to gather these persons is not to be understood of his divine will, or of his free will as God; *for who hath resisted his will?* this cannot be hindered nor made void; *he hath done whatsoever he pleased;* but of his human will, or of his will as man; which though not contrary to the divine will, but subordinate to it, yet not always the same with it, nor always fulfilled. He speaks here as a man and *minister of the circumcision*, and expresses a human affection for the inhabitants of Jerusalem, and a human wish or will for their temporal good, instances of which human affection and will may be observed

in Mark x. 21, Luke xix. 41, and xxii. 42. Besides, this will of gathering the Jews to him was in him, and expressed by him at certain several times, by intervals, and therefore he says, *How often would I have gathered*, &c. Whereas the divine will is one continued invariable and unchangeable will, is always the same, and never begins or ceases to be, and to which such an expression as this is inapplicable; and therefore this passage of Scripture does not contradict the absolute and sovereign will of God in the distinguishing acts of it, respecting election and reprobation.

4. That the persons whom Christ would have gathered are not represented as being *unwilling* to be gathered; but their rulers were not willing that they should. The opposition and resistance to the will of Christ, were not made by the people, but by their governors. The common people seemed inclined to attend the ministry of Christ, as appears from the vast crowds which, at different times and places, followed him; but the chief priests and rulers did all they could to hinder the collection of them to him; and their belief in him as the Messiah, by traducing his character, miracles, and doctrines, and by passing an act that whosoever confessed him should be put out of the synagogue; so that the obvious meaning of the text is the same with that of ver. 13, where our Lord says, *Wo unto you, scribes and Pharisees, hypocrites; for ye shut up the kingdom of heaven against men; for ye neither go in yourselves, neither suffer ye them that are entering to go in*; and consequently is no proof of men's resisting the operations of the Spirit and grace of God, but of obstructions and discouragements thrown in the way of attendance on the external ministry of the word.

5. That in order to set aside and overthrow the doctrines of the election, reprobation, and particular redemption, it should be proved that Christ, as God, would have gathered, not Jerusalem and the inhabitants thereof only, but all mankind, even such as are not eventually saved, and that in a spiritual saving way and manner to himself, of which there is not the least intimation in this text; and in order to establish the resistibility of God's Grace, by the perverse will of man, so as to become of no effect, it should be proved that Christ would have savingly converted these persons, and they would not be converted; and that he bestowed the same grace upon them he does bestow on others who are converted; whereas the sum of this passage lies in these few words, that Christ, as man, out of a compassionate regard

for the people of the Jews, to whom he was sent, would have gathered them together under his ministry, and have instructed them in the knowledge of himself as the Messiah; which, if they had only nationally received, would have secured them as chickens under the hen from impending judgments which afterwards fell upon them; but their governors, and not they, would not, that is, would not suffer them to be collected together in such a manner, and hindered all they could, their giving any credit to him as the Messiah; though had it been said *and they would not*, it would only have been a most sad instance of the perverseness of the will of man, which often opposes his temporal as well as his spiritual good.

The next verse is Acts 7:51. "Ye stiff-necked and uncircumcised in heart and ears, ye do always resist the Holy Ghost; as your fathers did, so do ye." This verse is supposed to be inconsistent with irresistible grace, and to imply therefore that man has ability to convert himself.

In reply it may be said that of course the workings of the Holy Spirit in some circumstances can be resisted. What the opponents must show is that the intention of the Holy Spirit to convert a particular individual can be resisted. Not all of the Spirit's workings aim at the conversion of someone. There is no evidence in Acts 7 that the Holy Spirit was trying to convert Stephen's persecutors. They were stiff-necked and uncircumcised in heart. They give no evidence of having even what the Arminians call sufficient grace to accept Christ by free will. They are hardened against God and resist the Spirit as he directs Stephen what to say. There is no reference in the chapter to any internal working of the Spirit in the hearts of the Pharisees. They resisted the Spirit as he worked in Stephen.

Suppose, contrary to the tone of the whole chapter, that the Spirit actually intended to regenerate these Pharisees, or some of them. The Arminians would then have to show that these persons were not later regenerated. It is clear from Scripture that often God prepares a man for conversion through prior vicissitudes. The man at first resists. But in the fulness of time, God regenerates him. As a matter of fact, though it is not mentioned in this chapter, this could have been God's intention with respect to the young man who guarded the Pharisees' clothes while the were stoning Stephen. Young Saul resisted, along with the others. But he did not so resist that the Spirit was compelled to capitulate. It was not yet the moment for Paul's conversion, but nonetheless God was working irresistibly. In general, although it is quite improbable that the Pharisees of this chapter were ever converted, the Arminians would have to prove two points before they could use such a verse as this. They would have to prove that the particular working of the Spirit was for the purpose of regenerating a man, and that the man was never regenerated. These two things cannot both be proved.

In the discussion of Deuteronomy 5:29 above there was an oblique anticipation of a New Testament verse that seems to say that God wants to save all men but that he does not have the power or ability to do so. That is, the verse supposedly asserts free will, and denies omnipotence. While John Gill examines many verses throughout both Testaments, this will be the last included here. And for this last again John Gill will be quoted in entirety.

> The Lord is not slack concerning his promise (as some men count slackness), but is longsuffering to us-ward, not willing that any should perish, but that all should come to repentance. —2 Peter iii. 9.
>
> This scripture appears among those which are said to be very many clear and express ones for the doctrine of universal redemption; and it is observed, "that *tines*, opposed to *pantes*, is a distributive of all, and, therefore, signifies, God is not willing that any one of the whole rank of men should perish." But,
>
> 1. It is not true that God is not willing any one individual of the human race should perish, since he has *made* and appointed *the wicked for the day* of evil, even *ungodly men*, who are *for-*

140

ordained to this condemnation, such as are *vessels of wrath fitted for destruction*; yea, there are some t whom *God sends strong delusions, that they may believe a lie, that they all might be damned*; and others *whose judgment now of a long time lingereth not and their damnation slumbereth not*. Nor is it his will that all men, in this large sense, should come to repentance, since he withholds from many both the means and grace of repentance; and though it is his will of precept, that all to whom the preaching of the Gospel is vouchsafed should repent, yet it is not his purposing, determining will, to bring them all to repentance, *for who hath resisted his will?*

2. It is very true that *tines*, any, being opposed to *pantes*, all, is a distributive of it; but then both the *any* and the *all* are to be limited and restrained by *us*, to whom God is long-suffering; God is not willing that any more should not perish, and is willing that no more should come to repentance than the *us* to whom his long-suffering is salvation. The key, therefore, to open this text lies in these words *eis emas, to us-ward*, or *for our sake;* for these are the persons God would not have any of them perish, but would have them all come to repentance. It will be proper, therefore,

3. To enquire who these are. It is evident that they are distinguished from the scoffers mocking at the promise of Christ's coming, ver. 3, 4, are called beloved, ver. 1, 8, 14, 17, which is to be understood either of their being beloved by God, with an everlasting and unchangeable love, or of their being beloved as brethren by the apostle and other saints; neither of which is true of all mankind. Besides, the design of the words is to establish the saints in, and comfort them with the coming of Christ, until which, God was long-suffering towards them, and which they were to account salvation, ver. 15. Add to this, that the apostle manifestly designs a company or society to which he belonged, and of which he was a part, and so can mean no other than such who were chosen of God, redeemed from among men, and called out of darkness into marvellous light; and such were the persons the apostle writes to. Some copies read the words *di umas, for your sakes;* so the Alexandria MS, the Syriac version *mtlthkvn, for you,* or your sakes; the same way the Ethiopic. Now these persons were such who were *elect, according to the foreknowledge of God the Father, through sanctification of the Spirit unto obedience, and sprinkling of the blood of Jesus*

141

Christ; and such, as these, or who belong to the same election of grace they did, God is unwilling that any of them should perish, but wills that all of them should have repentance unto life; and, therefore, he waits to be gracious to them, and defers the second coming of Christ. The case stands thus: there was a promise of Christ's second coming, to judge the world, delivered out; it was expected that this would have been very quickly, whereas it has been a long time deferred. Hence scoffers shall arise in the last days, charging the Lord with slackness and dilatoriness concerning his promise, though he is not slack with respect to it, but is long-suffering towards his elect, waiting till their number is completed in effectual vocation, and for their sakes bears with all the idolatry, superstition, and profaneness that are in the world; but when the last man that belongs to that number is called, he will stay no longer, but descend in flames of fire, take his own elect to himself, and burn up the world and the wicked in it.

4. It is indeed said, "that the apostle, by *the elect*, to whom he writes, does not mean men absolutely designed for eternal happiness, but only men professing Christianity, or such as were visible members of the church of Christ: since he calls upon them to *make* their *calling and election sure*, exhorts them to watchfulness, seeing their *adversary the devil goes about seeking whom he may devour*, and to *beware lest* they *fall from their own steadfastness;* yea, he speaks of some of them as having *forsaken the right way;* and also prophesies that *false teachers should make merchandize of them*, neither of which, it is observed, can be supposed of men absolutely elected to salvation; and, also that the church at Babylon was elected, together with these persons, which could not be known and said of all its members." To all of which I reply, that calling upon them to make their election sure, does not suppose it to be a precarious and conditional one, as I have shown in a preceding section; that exhortations to sobriety, and vigilance against Satan, and cautions about falling, are pertinent to such who are absolutely elected to salvation; for, though Satan cannot devour them, he may greatly distress them; and, though they shall not finally and totally fall from the grace of God, yet they may fall from some degree of steadfastness, both as to the doctrine and grace of faith, which may be to their detriment as well as to the dishonour of God: that it is not true, that the apostle speaks of

any of these elect he writes to, that they had *forsaken the right way*, but of some other persons; and though he prophesies that *false teachers* should *make merchandize* of them, the mean-is, that, by their fine words and fair speeches, they should be able to draw money out of their pockets, not that they should destroy the grace of God wrought in their hearts. As to the church at Babylon being said to be elected with them, the apostle might say this of the church in general, as he does, in a judgment of charity, of the church at Thessalonica, and others, though every member of it in particular was not elected to salvation, without any prejudice to the doctrine of absolute election. Besides, the persons he writes to were not visible members of any one particular church or community, professing Christianity, but were strangers scattered abroad in several parts of the world, and were such who had *obtained like precious faith* with the apostles, and is a strong evidence of their being men absolutely designed for eternal happiness. And whereas it is suggested, that these persons were come to repentance, and therefore cannot be the same to whom God is longsuffering, that they might come to repentance; I answer, that though they are not the same individual persons, yet are such who belong to the same body and number of the elect, on whom the Lord waits, and to whom he is longsuffering, until they are all brought to partake of this grace, having determined that not one of them should ever perish.

5. Hence it follows, that these words do not furnish out any argument in favour of universal redemption, nor do they militate against absolute election and reprobation, or unfrustrable grace in conversion; but on the contrary, maintain and establish them, since it appears to be the will of God, that not one of those he has chosen in Christ, given to him, and for whom he died, shall ever perish; and, inasmuch as evangelical repentance is neces-sary for them, and they cannot come at it of themselves, he freely bestows it on them, and, by his unfrustrable grace, works it in them; and, until this is done unto and upon every one of them, he keeps the world in being, which is *reserved unto fire, against the day of judgment, and perdition of ungodly men.*

Without further exegetical details another Baptist, who on some points had an even better understanding of the Scripture than John Gill, may be mentioned. He is one a

143

little nearer our own time, and a great example of preaching the gospel of grace with power from week to week. This man is Charles Haddon Spurgeon. Unfortunately some editions of his sermons have been edited so as to remove his strong Calvinistic statements. It is better to get and read the originals. In *The Early Years*, not a sermon but a part of Spurgeon's *Autobiography*, John Anderson is quoted: "Mr. Spurgeon is a Calvinist, which few of the dissenting ministers in London now are. He preaches salvation, not of man's free will, but of the Lord's *good will*, which few in London, it is to be feared, now do." Spurgeon himself, in his sermon, "Free Will — a Slave," says, "The error of Arminianism is not that it holds the Biblical doctrine of responsibility, but that it equates this doctrine with an unbiblical doctrine of free will. . . . Man, being fallen, his will cannot be neutral or 'free' to act contrary to his nature. 'Free will' has carried many souls to hell, but never a soul to heaven yet." Highly recommended for reading is *The Forgotten Spurgeon*, by Iain H. Murray (The Banner of Truth Trust, 1966).

Now, for a summation, this chapter has shown that the doctrine of free will is an imposition of false philosophy on the Scripture, such that the doctrine of salvation by grace is seriously distorted. It has also been shown that the Protestant Reformation in its return to the Scripture after a millennium of superstition uniformly rejected the popish and heathen doctrine of free will; but that a century after the Reformation this false doctrine recaptured a section of the non-romish churches. Finally, the Arminian misinterpretations of a number of verses have been exposed, so that it is clear that Arminianism is anti-scriptural, but that Calvinism is completely true to the Bible.

Chapter Seven

EPILOGUE

After Moses rescued his people from slavery, God granted them a great revival of true religion. To be sure, they soon sinned before the golden calf, but by the time of Moses' death the nation as a community exhibited the pure worship of Jehovah. This high level of spirituality continued throughout the lifetime of Joshua, for "the people served the Lord all the days of Joshua, and all the days of the elders that outlived Joshua, who had seen all the great works of the Lord, that he did for Israel" (Judges 2:7). Then deterioration set in, "and there arose another generation after them, which knew not the Lord, nor yet the works he had done for Israel. And the children of Israel did evil in the sight of the Lord, and served Baalim. And they forsook the Lord God of their fathers . . . and followed other gods . . . and provoked the Lord to anger" (Judges 2:10-12).

Then followed a period of ups and downs, short ups and long downs, for several centuries. Samuel in a sense may be called the forerunner of David, under whom the people in large numbers returned to God. This great revival of worship culminated in Solomon's building the Temple. Then came rebellion with its sorry history in the north and the slower but equally fatal apostasy in the south.

The captivity chastened the people somewhat, and under Ezra and Nehemiah they once more obeyed God. But not for long. By the time of Christ the Pharisees systematically misinterpreted the Law and the Sadducees insisted on being modern and relevant to their times. Only a few awaited the consolation of Israel.

Through the Apostle Paul God was pleased to make his salvation known to the Gentiles. For four centuries the Pauline impetus continued, in some theological respects reaching a higher level at the end than at the beginning, but in other respects marred by the continuance of pagan customs that eventually corrupted the forms of worship.

Then came a thousand years of ignorance, superstition, and immorality.

After the first faint glimmerings of Wycliffe and Huss, the clear light of day dawned with Zwingli, Luther, Calvin, Knox, and the other reformers. Though suppressed by fire and sword in many places, the Gospel was made known more fully than ever before — excepting only the preaching of the Apostles themselves. This happy condition continued to its culmination in the Westminster Confession of 1647. although by that time Arminius had begun his evil work. From then on the history of the Christian churches has resembled the period of the Judges—short ups and long downs.

Today the most numerous, the most visible, and the best advertized groups that oppose total apostasy retain very little Reformation theology. Unlike the Westminster Confession with its thirty-three chapters, their official faith is exhausted in a half-dozen articles; and when they preach beyond these they are anything but Calvinistic. Men like Spurgeon are hard, if not impossible, to find. Perhaps Martin Lloyd Jones is the nearest approach. J. L. Packer and other contributors to the symposia edited by Carl F. H. Henry, as well as some other scholars are known in learned circles. No doubt seven thousand of lesser stature have not bowed the knee to Baal. But there is no Elijah, and the reformed church is only a remnant.

146

Only in such an atmosphere of deterioration could the following piece of immorality have occurred. A little before the middle of the century, in a controversial situation, a gentleman remonstrated with me: Believe predestination, if you want to; but don't let people know you believe it. Such was the worldly-wise, hypocritical advice of an American fundamentalist leader. But as bad as the personal recommendation of hypocrisy is the evidence of how far American fundamentalism has fallen away from the light of the Protestant Reformation. There are many ministers, who say they believe the Bible, and yet question whether predestination should be preached to their congregations, even if true.

Predestination is such a difficult doctrine, so the objection goes, and in fact such a controversial doctrine that perhaps it would be better not to mention it. Strange it is that anyone makes this objection, if he has any idea of how the doctrine permeates the Bible from cover to cover. But the objection is indeed made. Clever evangelists, whose facility of expression is exceeded only by their misunderstanding of Scripture, have frequently used the illustration of the sheep and the giraffe. Several times I have heard a person say, Christ told us to feed his sheep—he did not say to feed his giraffes. The idea is that grass is on the ground and represents the easiest of doctrinal teaching. The material is on a kindergarten or Sunday School level. Leaves in the trees, which only giraffes or geniuses can reach, represent very difficult teaching, and if this is all there were to eat, the sheep would starve. But giraffes would not starve even if the trees were denuded, so long as there was plenty of grass. Such is the idea of the illustration; but such is not the idea of the Bible.

The Bible of course endorses feeding milk to babies. The simplest truths are to be taught to young Christians. Faith and repentance are said to be first principles; they are milk for babies. Even so, it is not clear that the doctrine of justification by faith and the doctrine of repentance are so simple and easy as the objectors would wish. After all, they depend on the doctrine of predestination with all the Scripture quoted in the present book. Some evangelists think that "Ye must be born again," is an easy doctrine; but learned Nicodemus found it too difficult to understand. Nor do the evangelists themselves succeed in making it simple for the uneducated. Popular evangelists might also wish to preach the Deity of Christ; but as this involves the doctrine of the Trinity and the Chalcedonian creed, it cannot be said to be a very simple and easy doctrine. In fact, predestination is much simpler and easier. Predestination is very easy to understand. The real trouble is that the natural man does not like it.

The death of Christ, the Atonement, or as it is better named, the Satisfaction must form a good part of evangelistic preaching. But is this very easy? I have heard many evangelists preach on the death of Christ without mentioning that Christ's death satisfied the justice of his Father. These evangelists may have preached something simple, but they simplified by omitting the essential part. The principle of being simple is a dangerous and unscriptural principle.

It is so because, whatever doctrines may be milk for babies, the Bible does not recommend that our teaching end with them. Hebrews 5:12–6:3 condemns the desire to remain on a Sunday School or primary level. People who remain satisfied with the elementary doctrines are "ununskillful in the word of righteousness"; and God commands them to rise from milk to strong meat, "not laying again the foundation of repentance . . . faith . . . the doctrine of baptisms and of the laying on of hands, and of the resurrection of the dead, and of eternal judgment," but God commands us to "go on unto perfection."

148

Even more clearly Christ's last command brings into awful condemnation those who wish to silence the preaching of predestination. "Go ye therefore and teach all nations . . . teaching them to observe all things whatsoever I have commanded you." Christ did not say, Teach all things except some difficult, distasteful, controversial, advanced, college-level, giraffe-like doctrines.

Evangelists and preachers who disobey Christ's command by omitting large and important sections of the Bible from their preaching are guilty of the blood of their people. Paul was not guilty. He said in Acts 20:26-27, "I am pure from the blood of all men, for I have not shunned to declare unto you all the counsel of God." The large modern denominations are today apostate because disobedient preachers have shunned to declare all the counsel of God. Predestination was silenced, total depravity was softened, regeneration was misunderstod, the Virgin Birth was denied, the Bible was reduced to myth, and the so-called Christian nations became secular.

If, now, we hope to shake the nations again as Luther and Calvin did, we must return to preaching all the counsel of God. If, on the other hand, this hope seems unfounded, and like Jeremiah we must preach to those who will not obey, still Christ has commanded us to teach all things revealed. Jerome Zanchius, near the end of his book on *Absolute Predestination*, lists some reasons for preaching the doctrine. First, he says, without it we cannot form just and becoming ideas of God. Foreknowledge, perfection, omnipotence, and sovereign grace must be abandoned, if predestination is denied. Second, to expand the last named of God's characteristics, the grace of God cannot be maintained without predestination. "There neither is nor can be any medium between predestinating grace and salvation by human merit." Third, by the preaching of predestination man is duly humbled and God alone is exalted. "Conversion and salvation must, in the very nature of the case, be wrought and effected either by ourselves alone, or by ourselves and God together, or *solely by God himself*. The Pelagians were for the first. The Arminians are for the second. True believers are for the last." An inquisitive reader may wish to get his book and see the remainder of his nine reasons.

But the sum of all reasons is that God commands us to teach the world all that he has revealed in his Word. Let no one disobey.

Part Two

PREDESTINATION IN THE OLD TESTAMENT

This study is a survey of what the Old Testament says about predestination. Even an Arminian knows that the New Testament uses the word several times, but many Christians think that the Old Testament says little or nothing at all about it. On the contrary, the Old Testament asserts the doctrine pervasively and explicitly. In particular, one will find there the two or three main points on which the Arminians argue most strenuously. One of these is the Arminian assertion of free will in opposition to Luther's and Calvin's denial of free will. But underlying this are two more fundamental doctrines: election and reprobation. Calvinists believe both; Arminians believe neither. That is to say, Calvinists believe that God is the cause both of sin and of salvation, while Arminians deny that God is the cause of either one. Yet the double denial makes a strange combination because one might think that those who dislike the idea of reprobation would be quite happy with the idea of election. But the whole matter is somewhat complicated, and no one can make the least progress without examining the biblical details.

The following survey of the details is not exhaustive, though it may be exhausting. Its extensiveness is justified by the widespread lack of awareness of how pervasive and how explicit these doctrines are in the Old Testament. If the reader cannot plunge through it all in one sitting, he can at least consult these references when preparing to teach a Sunday school lesson on a certain book, or when puzzled as he reads this or that chapter for his devotions.

There is also a particular contemporary value, a value that

no doubt has been and no doubt will be repeated in other situations. Recently Clark H. Pinnock has edited a book, *Grace Unlimited*. The title is somewhat strange, for the book defends a kind of grace that is not only limited, but actually frustrated by man's free will. To defend the thesis of a limited and frustrated grace, chapter six of the Pinnock book, written by David J. A. Clines, a lecturer in the University of Sheffield, England, proposes to study "Predestination in the Old Testament." The chapter opens with a most excellent statement on method. First it warns against two errors: "We may fail to see the whole range of the biblical revelation on the subject because *we* [italics his] have chosen the categories and terms that are going to count." Second, we may not have the correct focus and so distort relative values. Then positively the author, repeating the idea of "the whole range of the biblical revelation," advises us "to look at the biblical teaching as a whole," and to this end "to consider the parts of the Bible individually—at least to begin with."

This is an excellent statement of method. But Mr. Clines did not follow it. He began with Abraham instead of with Genesis 1:1. He later returns to the early chapters of Genesis for a few scattered points. Then he skips to Proverbs! All from Exodus through the Psalms is omitted, with the exception of sparse references as he discusses later books. After Proverbs he spends three pages on Ecclesiastes, and in pages 120-122 he covers *The Prophetic Literature,* adding less than two pages on *Other Old Testament Literature.* He has nothing, or virtually nothing, on Job, Psalms, nor on Exodus to Ruth, nor on Ezekiel. These extensive omissions contain a great deal of material that flatly contradicts the position of the Pinnock book.[1]

_____

[1]The general reading public may be well impressed by the Pinnock book for two reasons. First, the academic pedigree of the authors, summarized on pp. 9, 10, is impressive. Second, the style and the sincerity of the writers is

Pinnock's book is a passing phenomenon. But the ideas in it will be expressed in future books as they have been in earlier books. Hence, as the subject matter is of perennial interest to Bible students, the value of the present study is, hopefully, of more than contemporary importance. Once again, this is not an exhaustive study, but the references are more than a small sample.

The first Old Testament allusion to predestination is Genesis 1:1, "In the beginning God created the heavens and the earth."

The word *predestination* does not occur in this verse. Neither does the word Trinity occur anywhere in the Bible.

---

attractive. Such characteristics can win acceptance for the conclusions from those who have no other basis for judging. Now, in spite of the academic pedigree, chapter six has already been proved deficient in scholarship. Its omissions are unjustifiably extensive.

Certain other deficiencies, which many readers will fail to note, may well be mentioned as a warning against hasty approval. Page 263 says, "Stoicism did not produce a consistent view of freedom because of its atomistic-deterministic worldview." The truth is that the Stoics were not atomists. If the author so misunderstands his supportive material in Stoicism, it is at least possible that he misinterprets the Scripture as well.

Page 200 says, *"L'Homme* [by Descartes] was the first major total mechanistic physiological model of man in modern times. *(Meditations on the First Philosophy. . .)."* The truth is that Descartes was not a mechanist: he held that the volition of the soul could violate physical law; i.e., he excepted man (L'homme) from the mechanism of the remainder of the universe.

Page 207, note 10, says, "Some examples of such systems are: (1) Democritean physics, that is, classical Greek physics." The truth is that Democritean physics was not classical Greek physics. Before Democritus, i.e., Thales to Anaxagoras, it had of course not yet been formulated; and after Democritus it was explicitly rejected by Plato, Aristotle, the Stoics, and even by the Epicureans.

Finally, two of the authors make the same mistake in Greek grammar, and a third barely escapes it. Pages 182 and 200, discussing Ephesians 2:8, claim that the neuter demonstrative pronoun cannot refer to faith because faith is feminine, and pronouns must agree in gender with their referents. The truth is that the authors are unaware that feminine abstract nouns frequently take the neuter in these constructions. Their logic is also poor, for if the demonstrative refers to all salvation, it must include faith as a part, so that faith remains a gift of God, contrary to the authors' desires.

153

Yet the Bible teaches both. No sermon, no confession of faith, no book on theology can restrict itself to the precise wording of the Bible. If the Bible says that Shechem is north of Jerusalem, and if it also says that Beersheba is south of Jerusalem, we can conclude that Beersheba is south of Shechem, even if the Bible does not say so. The Scripture invites us to compare one passage with another and to draw the consequences. With reference to Genesis 1:1, the idea of creation, explained in many later verses, justifies certain conclusions that bear on the doctrine of predestination.

There are many verses later in Scripture, which, when put together, show that God created the universe out of nothing. One such verse comes quickly: "God said, let there be light, and there was light." Light appeared instantaneously by divine *fiat*, by divine command. Later on God formed the body of Adam out of earth, but then he breathed life into the clay.

Creation *ex nihilo*, out of nothing, implies two things. First there was no antecedent power to stimulate God; there was no one to suggest plans to God, or to suggest alterations to the plans God had; still less could anyone defeat God's purposes. God was alone. He could do as he pleased.

In the second place, after God created something, the thing had no authority to complain, Why hast thou made me thus? A wren has no right to complain that it is not an elephant. God had decided to create a *world*, and a world by definition includes differences. The different things have no *right* to hold God responsible for the qualities they have or the qualities they lack. God is responsible to no one. He distributed wings, legs, horns, and minds just as it suited him to. No one has any claim on God.

Many of the items in the preceding paragraph are stated in more or less detail throughout the Bible. But they are included in the concepts of creation. Creation implies the complete control of the sovereign Creator over the dependent creature.

And complete control is predestination. Thus the Bible's very first sentence reveals the doctrine here to be studied.

Now, Arminians, at least those who have escaped the contamination of liberalism, believe in creation. But they fail to see what it means. They suppose, particularly in the case of men, if not of angels, that once a being is created, he, she, or it can legitimately claim that God is obliged to treat him as he wants to be treated, rather than as God decides to treat him. Man has rights that God must respect. Quite the contrary, however, man has no rights in opposition to God. Whatever rights a man has, though the term *rights* is hardly proper, as was the case with qualities, are those God decides to give him. God as creator can give, withhold, or retake any rights as he pleases. Whatever he gives to man is a gift and not a debt. No one has any claims over the Creator. Let us see how carefully the Old Testament spells this out.

At this point the author must choose between two methods of procedure. One way would be to collect all the passages on creation, then pass to another topic and collect all the passages relating to God's control of kings, and then to regeneration and the gift of faith. All these topics could be arranged in a somewhat logical order.

The other method, less logical, is to proceed from Genesis one, to Genesis two, and on to Malachi four. This would bring into juxtaposition passages that have different contents. In spite of its somewhat haphazard results, this method will be followed here because (1) the method will show the development of the doctrine from the time of Adam, Abraham, and Moses on to the end, (2) it will be more in keeping with the necessary reliance on exegesis, and (3) it will allow the reader, a few weeks after he has read the material, to find easily a verse that troubles his memory.

The second passage, after Genesis 1:1, that bears on the subject to a degree is Genesis 2:16-17. The idea here is a particular example of one of creation's implications. The dis-

155

cussion of creation, just above, insisted that man has no rights in opposition to God. Here we see God imposing obligations on man. "The Lord God *commanded* . . . thou mayest freely eat . . . but [of another tree] thou shalt not eat." What God commanded was not determined by Adam's likes and dislikes.

One might next cite the account of the flood to show God's control over the forces of nature. More profoundly nature has no forces: they are God's forces and he sends floods and earthquakes as he pleases. But since Arminians do not generally contest God's control of inanimate nature, this point needs little emphasis.

Yet when the forces of inanimate nature and human nature combine to produce historical events, the Arminian agrees only with hesitation. In Genesis 12:1ff. God makes certain promises to Abraham. God, not Abraham, will make Abraham's descendants a great nation. God will bless and curse. "Unto thy seed," God says in Genesis 12:7, "will I give this land." Then in Genesis 15:1 further promises are made. In particular God promises that Abraham shall have an heir, and a numerous posterity (15:4, 5). More to the point, God in Genesis 17:1 declares that he is almighty. That is, he can do anything he wishes to. Now, the Arminians will admit that God can work on an elderly woman's body so that she can bear a son. But if God can do anything, he can also cause Abraham to choose to migrate to Palestine and later cause Jacob to migrate to Egypt so as to fulfill the prophecy of Geneses 15:13. In view of such prophecies, what answer must be given to the question, Was it possible for Jacob to will never to descend into Egypt? Can man will to prevent God's predictions from coming to pass? Must not man will to fulfill them?

It may seem odd at first, but does not God's promise to Abraham of numerous descendants imply that Abraham could not have chosen to commit suicide before he had begotten a son? If God promised to give Abraham's seed the land of Palestine, then it was certain that Abraham would have children. He had no free will by which to choose to commit suicide. God controlled Abraham's will so that he could not choose otherwise.

Does it seem far-fetched to say that God controls men's wills? Consider another verse. Abraham had moved south to Gerar, in the kingdom of Abimelech. Abimelech immediately became enamored of Sarah's beauty. He took her. God then spoke to the king in a dream: "The woman which thou hast taken, she is a man's wife. But Abimelech had not come near her. . . . She herself said, He [Abraham] is my brother. In the integrity of my heart and innocency of my hands have I done this. And God said . . . I know . . . for I also withheld thee from sinning against me, therefore suffered I thee not to touch her" (Gen. 20:3-6).

This is something the Arminians do not understand, nor can they fit it into their theology. Abimelech had no free will. He simply could not have chosen to lie with Sarah that night because God controlled his will and caused him to refrain. A *free* will, of course, is one that is *determined* by nothing. It is equally able to make either of two incompatible choices. But God determined Abimelech not to make the one choice; he caused him to make the other.

God can and does control the wills or choices of men because he is almighty. It is not necessary to list all the verses in which divine omnipotence is asserted. But one which comes shortly after Genesis 17:1 is Genesis 28:3. Surely anyone who reads the Old Testament halfway through is forced to admit that it teaches divine omnipotence. Nothing can interfere with God's decisions. Created objects are his creations; he can turn them this way or that as he pleases.

One further verse in Genesis, however, must be listed because it is one of the clearest Calvinistic and anti-Arminian verses in the whole Bible. After the death of Jacob,

Joseph's brethren were afraid that Joseph might take vengeance on them for their earlier misdeeds. To them Joseph replied, "Ye thought evil against me, but God meant it unto good, to bring to pass, as it is this day, to save much people alive" (Gen. 50:20). The jealous brothers had earlier considered murdering Joseph, but they changed their minds and sold him into slavery. Their intentions were evil; but God had controlled their wills. They simply could not have remained firm in their decision to kill Joseph because God had decreed to send Joseph to Egypt for the purpose of later saving that family from starvation. The brothers decided to sell Joseph. God controlled their decision. They were not free to will his death, nor to let him go, either. So ends Genesis.

Since Dr. Clines in the Pinnock volume omits everything from Exodus to Proverbs, here is the only place to comment on his arguments about Genesis. On page 112, concerning Abraham, and presumably Joseph too, he writes, "The story is focused . . . on the hazards which the promise faces. . . . It is from the tension between the promise and the reality of life that the story gains its momentum. So the predestination is not the absolutely determinative factor in what happens." That the poignancy and tension of the story depends on the realities of life may well be granted; but the logic by which the writer draws his conclusion cannot be granted. Even if the clear Calvinistic verses had been omitted from the story, it would still be a fallacy to conclude, "So predestination is not absolutely determinative." The absence from the story of the determinative factor would be no proof of its absence from reality. Could we argue that predestination is a false doctrine because II Chronicles 25:12 does not mention it? This Arminian argument from silence is repeated on page 113, where the author gives an all-too-brief glance at Adam, Cain, and the tower of Babel. He argues that the text does not mention the eternal decrees. Obviously the logic is fallacious. And furthermore, while II Chronicles 25:12 is indeed silent on the matter of predestination, Genesis is not silent.

After Genesis the book of Exodus emphasizes the doctrine of predestination in what Arminians might call its most virulent form. But regardless of Arminian objections, Exodus is so clearly Calvinistic, or Calvinists are so Exodusians, that the continued existence of Arminianism is a miracle of blindness.

The beginning of this material is Exodus 4:21, "And the Lord said to Moses . . . I will harden [Pharaoh's] heart, that he shall not let the people go." In view of the predictions in Exodus three and four, in which Pharaoh's refusal is predicted (3:19), and because of the explicit wording of 4:21, how can an Arminian say that Pharaoh was free to let the slaves go? If God hardened his heart, what possibility was there that he could do otherwise? Is not God omnipotent? Cannot omnipotence control the will of man? Arminians are likely to hedge and reply that God, since he is omnipotent, *can* control his creatures, but out of respect to their integrity he *will* not control them. But what Arminians say God would not do, the verse says God did.

Now it is a standard rule of theology that no doctrine should be based on a single verse. To avoid errors of interpretation a Christian must compare Scripture with Scripture and use as many verses as possible. In the case of predestination it is easy to accumulate verses; the only difficulty is finding them all. The particular assertion of the last verse quoted is repeated in Exodus 7:3. It says, "I will harden Pharaoh's heart." Suppose now that someone in desperation tries to reply, Well, God said, "I will"; but that is the future tense. Then he later changed his mind and didn't. This is indeed desperation. Aside from the fact that God never changes his mind, for he is eternally immutable, Exodus 7:13 tells us plainly that what God predicted he would do, he did: "He hardened [past tense] Pharaoh's heart."

Now, there are some verses in which this event is mentioned without indicating who did the hardening. Exodus 7:22 simply says, "Pharaoh's heart was hardened." Then with a sigh of relief the Arminian hurries on to Exodus 8:15 and 32. See, he says, "Pharaoh hardened his [own] heart." Some non-Christians might be more gleeful and say, "See, the Bible contradicts itself." The alleged contradiction, however, will soon disappear as the Arminian remark is considered.

A bit of statistics will improve the perspective. Exodus mentions the hardening of Pharaoh's heart eighteen times, to which may be added one other verse that applies to the Egyptians in general. Exodus 4:21; 7:3, 13; 9:12;10:1, 20, 27; 11:10; 14:4, 8 all say that the Lord hardened Pharaoh's heart. The extra verse says that the Lord hardened the hearts of the Egyptians (Exod. 14:17). This is eleven times out of nineteen. Five instances, 7;14, 22; 8:19; 9:7, 35, do not specify who hardened Pharaoh's heart. The other verses, three in number, 8:15, 32 and 9:32, say that Pharaoh hardened his heart. Who, then, in the face of the eleven statements that the Lord hardened Pharaoh's heart can deny that God is the cause of this hardening? Not only is this positive statement made three times more often, but it is made three times before the other statement is made once. After all, who runs Egypt—Pharaoh or God?

Well, in two different senses God and Pharaoh both run Egypt. And this fact, which many inconsistent Arminians would admit, shows how both God and Pharaoh can harden Pharaoh's heart.

The difficulties that Arminians encounter arise from their usually unexpressed idea that the relationship between God and his creature is essentially similar to that between two creatures. But if this is not true of personal relationships on a lower plane, it is exceedingly and outstandingly false on a higher. The relationship between a four-star general of the army and a subordinate is not that which obtains between two first-class privates. Much less is man's relation to man the same as man's relation to God. One man may persuade another to choose a course of action; he may by torture force a man to do something; but even this is not omnipotent control of the other's will. In the usual situation the person's will is obviously free from the other's. This is not the case between God and man. When Paul preached in Athens, if a New Testament reference be permitted in an Old Testament chapter, he said, "In him we live and move and have our being." The "we" does not refer to Paul and other Christians alone. It particularly refers to Paul and his pagan audience. The pagans lived and moved, thought and spoke, in God. Their minds and God's mind interpenetrated. The doctrine of omnipotence shows that God can control men's wills; the passage in Acts makes somewhat clearer how God controls men's wills. My toothache does not exist in your mind; and many of your thoughts do not exist in mine. But every thought of yours and mine alike is found in God's mind. This interpenetration at least clarifies to some degree the manner in which the Creator's mind controls his creatures' thoughts.

Before leaving Exodus and Pharaoh, we can see there some of God's purpose in hardening Pharaoh's heart. God always acts for a purpose. Exodus 9:16 says, "For this cause have I raised thee up, for to show in thee my power, and that my name may be declared throughout all the earth." If God had not hardened Pharaoh's heart, if Pharaoh's will had been free, he might have let the Israelites go, at least after two or three plagues. But in this case God's power in the other plagues would not have been manifested, nor the great deliverance at the Red Sea. In order to drown the Egyptian army, after the Israelites had passed through safely, God hardened Pharaoh's heart.

This idea of God's controlling the will and thoughts of men is not something rare or exceptional in the Bible. The next verse is Deuteronomy 2:30: "Sihon, King of Heshbon, would not let us pass by him; for the Lord thy God hardened his spirit and made his heart obstinate that he might deliver him into thy hand."

This differs from the case of Pharaoh in Exodus only by the absence of any statement that Sihon hardened his own spirit. Otherwise the verse asserts God's activity or causality and the purpose for which he made Sihon do what he did. Then Moses, in the passage, continues by declaring that God's purpose was fulfilled: Heshbon was totally destroyed and "only the cattle we took for a prey unto ourselves."

A final verse from Deuteronomy is very explicit; but a collateral verse that emphasizes God's sovereignty, though its application to predestination is only briefly touched on in one phrase, may first be mentioned. Deuteronomy 10:17 says, "For the Lord your God is God of gods and Lord of lords, a great God, a mighty and terrible, who regardeth not persons, nor taketh reward." An Arminian preacher could hardly be very enthusiastic in choosing this verse as the text for a sermon, though he could awkwardly insist that the idea of predestination is not prominent. The contrast, however, is that the Calvinistic preacher could enthusiastically use the verse for a series of sermons.

These previous verses have been instances in which the Lord caused certain people to think thoughts and make decisions to their own destruction. But consistent Arminians also dislike the idea that God causes people to think thoughts and make decisions for their own good. If the will is free, God can cause good inclinations as little as he can cause evil decisions. However, Deuteronomy 30:6 says, "The Lord thy God will circumcise thine heart . . . to love the Lord thy God with all thine heart, and with all thy soul, that thou mayest live."

Circumcision of the heart is presumably identical to regeneration in the New Testament. In any case the verse under discussion makes it clear that a great spiritual change is involved. This circumcision will cause them to love God with all their hearts, and will cause them "to return and obey the voice of the Lord." Circumcision is the cause; loving the

162

Lord is the result. This particular verse does not say that if they are not circumcised they cannot love God; though this idea is given elsewhere in the Bible. But it obviously says that God's act caused them to love him. And of course God chooses, determines, predestinates, or selects which persons he will circumcise. That this future tense may refer more to the Messianic age than to the time of Joshua does not detract from the present argument. Whether sooner or later, God produces in these people the volition of love.

It is impossible to list all the verses that bear upon the doctrine of predestination. Nor should too many verses be quoted that do nothing more than repeat a previous idea. For example, God's omnipotence, stated quite explicitly in Genesis, is stated just as clearly, but without much development, in Exodus 6:3; Numbers 24:4, 16; Ruth 1:20, 21 and more than two dozen times in Job. Such verses need not be quoted here unless they make some particular point. But the reader should be aware that this much of the doctrine of predestination is pervasive.

I Samuel 2:3, 6-9 seem to add a little bit. They say that God is a God of knowledge; he weighs the actions of men. He kills people and resurrects them. He keeps the feet of his saints. By themselves these verses do not seem to support the doctrine of predestination to any great degree. But one may surmise, and later verses will confirm it, that some of these predicted events, and the knowledge by which God predicts them, and God's employment of human agents in some cases, presupposes God's control of men's thoughts and volitions.

I Samuel itself gives more. In 12:22 it says, "It has pleased the Lord to make you his people." The reason the Jews could worship the Lord, as they did sometimes, was that God had chosen them. This did not depend on their volition. God is no respecter of persons, and the Israelites were not a great people, nor did they have any qualities that could determine God to choose them. His choice was simply his good pleasure. This resulted in their thinking, sometimes, that it was good to sacrifice as Moses commanded.

Of course the Israelites did not always have good thoughts, nor did they always worship God as Moses had prescribed. Why? I Samuel 16:14 says, "The Spirit of the Lord departed from Saul, and an evil spirit from the Lord troubled him. And Saul's servants said unto him, Behold now, an evil spirit from the Lord troubleth thee."

This surely must be a hard verse for Arminians to swallow. For the present purpose it is not necessary to decide whether or not Saul had ever been regenerated. In either case God took from Saul whatever divine wisdom he had been given to govern his people. The Spirit having departed, Saul was not free to think the good thoughts or to will the good actions of his early reign. Not only was he unable to do good, the Lord himself sent an evil spirit upon him and thus caused him to choose evil thoughts and actions. The idea that man has some personal integrity and freedom that God dare not violate is the reverse of what the Bible teaches. God predetermines a man's thoughts and volitions. It is not that Saul could not do good, if he so willed. The point is he could not so will. He was not free; he was under the power of an evil spirit that the Lord had sent him.

A similar instance is given in II Samuel 17:14: "Absalom and all the men of Israel said, the counsel of Hushai the Archite is better than the counsel of Ahithophel. For the Lord had appointed to defeat the good counsel of Ahithophel, to the intent that the Lord might bring evil upon Absalom." Notice the chain of purposes. God purposed to bring evil upon Absalom. To accomplish this he not only sent Hushai to Absalom's counsel chamber, but caused Absalom and all his men to decide that Hushai's bad counsel was better than Ahithophel's wise counsel. God controlled their thoughts. It was impossible for Absalom to think and decide otherwise, for God was controlling their minds "to the intent that the Lord might

164

bring evil upon Absalom." The situation is all the more convincing because it is a standard rule of warfare to follow up a victory immediately. But then General Bragg made the same mistake after Chickamauga. God predestinated his delay too.

Although the Pinnock book makes only an offhand reference to Samuel, Kings, and Chronicles, and gives them no serious consideration, the incidental remark directly contradicts what these books say. On page 123 Dr. Clines asserts that in the history of David "the story moves on the level of human intrigue . . . and the narrator does not pause to indicate where God's hand may be in this melee of incidents." This statement is false. The narrator not only "pauses," he explicitly shows God's hand in these events. The reason Absalom accepted Hushai's advice was that God had determined to defeat Absalom by this particular means. The case is the same with I Samuel 16:14, as has just been shown. God sent the evil spirit. The following paragraphs will now show other cases where Dr. Clines directly contradicts the Bible.

The same sort of situation is described in I Kings 22:20ff. The Lord had determined to kill Ahab. To do this God sent him a lying spirit to persuade Ahab to do battle at Ramoth-Gilead. Note that in verse 22, after the lying spirit, perhaps over-confidently, guaranteed to persuade Ahab, the Lord said, "Thou shalt persuade him and prevail also; go forth and do so."

The reader will remember that Ahab disguised himself so as not to attract the enemy's attention; but "a certain man drew a bow at a venture and smote the King of Israel. . . ." God controlled the flight of the arrow. He had as easily controlled Ahab's decision to go to war. Ahab could not possibly have willed otherwise.

II Chronicles 10:15 is another instance of the divine determination of a king's choice: "the cause was of God, that the Lord might perform his word"—his promise to Jeroboam.

165

Two more similar instances occur in II Chronicles. In 25:17-23 Amaziah's refusal to take Joash's warning seriously came from God. Then in a happier context, II Chronicles 36:22 reports that the Lord stirred up the spirit of Cyrus to favor the Jews. In both cases God determines what a man thinks, as well as what he does.

A leading Arminian of an earlier generation denied that God could so control man. D. D. Whedon's *The Freedom of the Will* (1864) is a standard work on the subject. Part II, section 3, chapter 4 (pp. 293 ff.) reads as follows:

"Predestination . . . is not only involved in endless difficulties and perplexities, but in meeting the demands of a rational theodicy and of Scripture interpretation . . . the text of Scripture can be naturally construed without owing it any obligations."

Strangely enough the book of 438 pages is almost completely devoid of scriptural references. It reminds me of a personal encounter. After quoting and explaining a dozen or more passages to a recalcitrant disputant, I finally challenged him to give me the verses on which he based his belief in free will. The poor fellow looked at me in stupefaction, and finally mumbled that he did not need any verses. The will is simply free. But to continue with Whedon's more scholarly attempt:

"The Divine Plan, as embraced in God's predetermination, is a scheme strictly embracing only the Divine Actions. Supposing that in the infinitely distant anterior 'timelessness' God is employed in selecting from all possible systems that which his wisdom best approves, the system which he is to be viewed as finally adopting is a *system consisting, properly and directly, of his own future actions* [ital. his]. Knowing indeed by the absolute perfection of his own attribute of omniscience all future possibilities . . . God does, in full foreknowledge of all results in the case, so plan all his own actions. . . . God's predeterminations of *his* own future action, or

166

course of action, are to be considered as so far *contingent*, as that their execution or coming into existence is conditioned upon the coming into existence of many presupposed free actions of finite agents, which are able not to be put forth."

The scope of the present publication does not include an examination of the underlying philosophy of this quotation. Those familiar with the history will recognize that it posits an 'Idea of Good' superior to and independent of the will of God. But let that pass. The important point is that Whedon here denies what the Bible asserts time and time again. Predestination does not terminate on God's actions. It is the actions and thoughts of men which he foreordains. No wonder there is virtually no appeal to Scripture anywhere in the book.

The appeal to Scripture in this study, though incomplete, is long and may seem tedious. Its purpose is to show how pervasive the doctrine of predestination is. Therefore the list continues.

Ezra 1:1 repeats II Chronicles 36:22: the Lord stirred up the spirit of Cyrus to make a proclamation. Ezra 6:22 declares that the Lord "turned the heart of the king of Assyria unto them." The next chapter adds, "the king granted him [Ezra] all his request, according to the hand of the Lord his God upon him." The last "him" probably means Ezra, and not the king; nevertheless it was the Lord who determined what the king would decide.

Since the term "freewill" occurs twice in this chapter, a consideration of such an "Arminian verse" will not be amiss. Ezra 7:13 is a decree of King Artaxerxes. It permitted all the Jews "which are minded of their own freewill to go up to Jerusalem, to go with thee." Verses 15 and 16 say that they may take their "freewill offerings" with them.

The matter of "freewill offerings" is easily disposed of. There are several other Old Testament verses that use this phrase. But they have nothing to do with the theory of free will. The Hebrew term, for "freewill" is an English word, means abundantly, spontaneously, voluntarily. It contrasts with the offerings that are prescribed by law, and which therefore are not spontaneous, nor even abundant. The question as to whether or not God controls the decision is entirely absent. So too in 7:13 the same Hebrew word is used. Even if the heathen king had used the English term "freewill", we would not be greatly impressed by his theology. Artaxerxes simply meant that if any Jew wanted to return to Jerusalem, he was free to go—free from royal restrictions. But Ezra, to indicate the inspired view of the matter, adds in 7:27, 28, "Blessed be the Lord . . . which hath put such a thing as this in the king's heart . . . and hath extended mercy unto me before the king." Ezra does not reflect on God's moving some Jews to return to Jerusalem, but he is very clear that God controlled Artaxerxes.

Next is the book of Job. If this book was written by or about someone who lived in the days of Abraham, we can see how early and how emphatically God revealed the principle of predestination. The Apostle Paul, however irrefragably he proclaimed it, was a late comer. Much in the book of Job can be called background material. Such passages do not make everything explicit, but they hardly make sense except on the Calvinistic doctrine.

For example, in chapter one Satan appears in heaven before God. They discuss the righteous Job. For the test described, "the Lord said unto Satan, Behold, all he hath is in thy power, only upon himself put not forth thy hand." When the ensuing disasters and tragic bereavements ensued, "Job sinned not, nor charged God foolishly." Then Satan asked to torment Job in his body, for said Satan, "Put forth thine hand now, and touch his bone and his flesh, and he will curse thee to thy face." To which God replied, "Behold, he is in thine hand, but save his life."

Arminians are usually quite content to have God "permit" things, evil things, to happen. They are not willing to say that God causes them to happen. And they are stirred to indignation if anyone says that God causes a man to choose evil. Calvinists ask, Can the former be maintained without the latter?

It may be noted in the first place that Satan himself regards his own torturing of Job as something done by God. "Put forth thy hand," says Satan, "and touch his flesh." Not to belabor this point, and to acknowledge that Satan was the immediate cause of Job's misery, and even to say that God "permitted" it all, the idea of permission hardly absolves God of the Arminian variety of responsibility. God knew what Satan would do; and God said, "Do it." The text itself underlines the point that Satan can do nothing without God's permission. The fact that Satan was God's hand is not something the Arminians can approve of.

But there is more. Even before chapter two, the Sabeans destroyed some of Job's children with the sword. Omit the fire of verse 16. The Chaldeans slew some other servants and stole the camels. In order to accomplish these things, the Sabeans and Chaldeans had to decide to do them. The chapter certainly suggests no doubt that Satan could effect these tragedies. Then he must have been able to control the volitions of these people. Let it be said once, and let it be said twice, that Satan could not have used the marauders unless God had given him permission. But the fact remains that Satan controlled what the Arminians regard as a free will. "Free" wills, however, are those that nothing causes.

Job 10:8-9 repeats an idea encountered before, and one which will be repeated on through the Old into the New Testament with increasing emphasis. The verses say, "Thine hands have fashioned me. . . . Thou hast made me as the clay." Since the implications of the Potter and the clay come out more strongly later on, we may here proceed to the next passage.

Job 14:5 reads, "his days are determined . . . thou hast appointed his bounds that he cannot pass." This very obviously

169

indicates that God controls the length of one's life. This much predestination does not worry our opponents. It is, however, one of the many details which together show that God governs all his creatures and all their actions. The reference to "bounds that he cannot pass" may also mean nothing more than the length of life. But if perchance, like Acts 17:26, it includes the "bounds of his habitation," the inference would be that God determines where a man chooses to live, so that he could not choose another place.

There are many passages which do not by themselves establish the full doctrine of predestination. The Arminians can rightly insist that an argument based on them is logically inconclusive. Nevertheless, so many details are enumerated here and there, that the description as a whole favors full predestination and is devoid of any hint to the contrary. For example, Job 15:14 teaches that babies are not born righteous, or even neutral, but definitely sinful. More compelling is Job 19:8-20. This passage indicates that God changed the thoughts and minds of Job's brethren, acquaintances, kinsfolk, maids, servants, children, and wife. Note that not only did God cause certain physical torments, but he caused the people mentioned to change their attitude toward Job. Nothing in this distressing situation occurred without the divine activity.

In 23:10 Job acknowledges that God will eventually bring him forth as gold; but it is nonetheless that these evils are what God desires (v. 13): "What his soul desires, even that he doeth; for he performeth the thing that is appointed for me . . . for God maketh my heart soft, and the Almighty troubleth me." In the first chapter Satan had asked permission to do these things; but Job recognizes that they are God's actions.

Another idea begins to emerge in Job 31:4, an idea that is clearly contrary to the doctrine of free will. The verse says, "Doth not he see my ways, and count all my steps?" At first sight it may seem that God, after being ignorant for a time, be-

170

gan to look at Job and count his steps. Thus God learned something he had not known before. This is why the sentence above says that another idea begins to emerge. The idea concerns God's knowledge. Later verses will give a more adequate account of God's knowledge, and then it will become evident that omniscience and free will cannot be made compatible.

Next it would be well to read Job 33:4-17, in which these phrases appear: "I also am formed out of clay . . . he marketh all my paths . . . he giveth not account of any of his matters . . he openeth the ears of men and sealeth their instruction that he may withdraw man from his purpose. . . ." Again the Scripture says that God is the Potter and we are the clay. He makes each of us into whatever sort of vessel he chooses. No one can call him to account; he is not responsible to us or to anyone else. If he pleases to change our purposes and choices, he does so.

If any man should try to hold God responsible, God answers (Job 38:4, 31), "Where wast thou when I laid the foundations of the earth; declare, if thou hast understanding. . . . Canst thou bind the sweet influences of the Pleiades or loose the bands of Orion?" It is not man's prerogative to reply against God. "Shall he that contendeth with the Almighty instruct him? He that reproveth God, let him answer it" (Job 40:2). These are not the words of a Calvinist addressing James Arminius and John Wesley. They are the words of God.

But perhaps the strongest verse, among all these strong verses, is Job 42:2. The King James Version reads, "I know that thou canst do everything, and that no thought can be withholden from thee." The American Standard Version of 1901 makes it a little clearer: "I know that thou canst do all things, and that no purpose of thine can be restrained." God can do all things. He can and does change man's thoughts. It was his purpose that Judas should choose to betray Christ.

171

Judas could not have chosen otherwise. His will was not free. Otherwise Judas could have ruined God's eternal plan and falsified all the prophecies. It was also God's purpose to change Paul's will. Paul could not have resisted the heavenly vision. Otherwise Paul would have been able to ruin God's plans for preaching the gospel to the Gentiles.

And all this theology was revealed to Job perhaps as early as 2000 B.C.

The Psalms contain a large number of sections that bear indirectly on predestination by teaching the sovereignty of God. These will be omitted here because an opponent would take refuge in their indirectness and refuse to see their implications. He would want something more explicit. Well, the Psalms provide such verses also. Yet the Calvinist will never renounce logic: if the Scripture implies something, that something must be accepted. If a college student in a Logic class complains about the age-old syllogism—all men are mortal, Socrates is a man, therefore Socrates is mortal—and remarks, "I agree that all men are mortal and that Socrates is a man, but you can't force on me that mere human logic which implies that Socrates is mortal," the professor must reply, if you do not grasp implication, you cannot understand anything, for nothing is clearer.

Hence, when Psalm 14 emphasizes total depravity: "They are corrupt . . . they are all together become filthy, there is none that doeth good, no, not one"; and when this is joined to Job 15:14 and 25:4, and later verses both in the Old Testament and the New, one sees that all people are totally alienated from God. Genesis 6:5 says that every imagination of the thoughts of his [man's] heart was only evil continually. The result is not simply that the natural man cannot do good; he cannot even want to. How then, as Job asked, can a man born of a woman be clean? The will of man must be changed; and only God can make a man clean. God must redirect his thoughts. The man himself is not free to do so. God, of course,

172

decides, chooses, predestinates whom he will cleanse.

Why should Arminians think that God cannot or will not alter a man's volitions? Psalm 33:6-11 says, "By the word of the Lord were the heavens made . . . he spake and it was done. . . . The Lord bringeth the counsel of the heathen to nought; he maketh the devices of the people of none effect." The Arminian will doubtless say that God sends pestilence, storms, or fire from heaven upon the armies of wicked kings, and thus brings their plans to nought. So he did. But cannot the Creator also defeat his enemies by causing them to make inefficient choices? If the Arminian should insist that these verses do not explicitly teach that God causes human volitions, what can he say about the next verse: "Blessed is the nation whose God is the Lord; and the people whom he hath chosen for his own inheritance." God chooses whom he will cleanse; God chooses who his heirs shall be. The heirs do not resist his choice because God controls their response. If this psalm is not sufficiently explicit, the next two, and especially the second, leave no loophole.

Psalm 51:10 does not touch upon regeneration, but upon an already regenerate man who has grievously sinned. He pleads, "Create in me a clean heart, O God, and renew a right spirit within me." David does not claim to be able to cleanse himself. This requires the omnipotent, creative power of God. The verb is the same as in Genesis 1:1, and in the matter of creation David can no more cause it, hinder it, or alter it in any way than could the original firmament. David also prays, "Renew a right spirit within me." Previously he had had adulterous and murderous thoughts. Now he asks God to change his mind so that never again would he so think. And though it breaks the order of verses, it is pertinent at this point to join Proverbs 20:9 with Job and with the Psalm: "Who can say, I have made my heart clean?" Only God can regenerate the mind, or change it after sin, and cause it to think holy thoughts. And if Arminians think any holy thoughts, they should thank God for them instead of boasting of their free will.

The next verse, Psalm 65:4, seems at first sight to be as explicit as any Calvinist could wish. Does it not say, "Blessed is the man whom thou choosest and causest to approach unto thee." Isn't God's causality in mercy stated here in the clearest terms? Well, not exactly. The word *cause* is not in the Hebrew. Not even the causative Hiphil form of the verb *approach* is in the text. It is the Piel form—a somewhat emphatic form, but not quite causative. Worse yet, it is here not so much emphatic as it is a way of turning an intransitive verb into a transitive one. The translation is, "Blessed is the man whom thou choosest and bringest unto thee." Nevertheless, if this is not such an explicit statement of causality as the Calvinist might wish for, it is still entirely too Calvinistic for the Arminian. Clearly and explicitly it says that God chooses certain people; and it also says that God brings these people to himself. If God brings them, they cannot refuse to be brought. The Psalm as a whole praises the omnipotence of God and his activities in many spheres. The subject is God's sovereignty, not his limitation.

Nothing could be more anti-scriptural than the exhortation of a very popular, contemporary evangelist. As a couple of hundred people came down the aisle to the front after the sermon, the evangelist addressed the fifteen thousand in their seats: You have prayed for these who now stand before me, he said, and that is good; you will pray for them tomorrow, and that is good; but there is no use of your praying for them now, *for not even God can help them*—they must decide by themselves. The wording here may not be absolutely verbatim, but the phrase underlined is precisely, word for word, what the evangelist said. David's religion and David's salvation were completely different.

Such explicit powerful verses as Psalm 65:4 make it proper to use the more indirect passages. Psalm 102:26-27 teaches

174

God's immutability. Now, if by free will a man could resist God's choosing and refuse to be brought to the holy temple, God would have to alter his plans. He would have to adjust himself to an independent force. He could not remain of the same mind. But Psalm 104:24, speaking of "how manifold are they works," says, "in wisdom hast thou made them all." It would not have been very wise to make a man who could disrupt his plans. The choice of whom he will regenerate, as well as the choice of men and actions to fulfill his prophecies, presupposes complete control. Otherwise Ruth could have left Naomi, returned with Orpah, and David would never have been king. Then there could have been no later Son of David to save his people from their sins.

Since the Arminians, inconsistently, allow God some control over his creation, the crux of the matter is located in the conflict between predestination and free will. God can and does cause earthquakes. Can God and does God control the volitions of human beings? The Arminians strongly assert man's independence of God. But the Scripture asserts the reverse. Whether a man's decision is good or evil, God causes him to make that choice.

Psalm 105:25 says, "He turned their heart to hate his people, to deal subtly with his servants." It may seem strange that God would cause anyone to hate his people. But it can seem strange to those only who either are ignorant of God's revelation or who reject it. The Psalm explicitly says that God turned their hearts to hatred, he made them think evil thoughts, he controlled their decisions.

Do not reply that God could but does not control all his creatures and all their actions. Psalm 115:3 says, "Our God is in the heavens, he hath done whatsoever he hath pleased." God wanted Ruth to be the great grandmother of David. So he did what he pleased. He not only altered Ruth's earlier Moabite thoughts, but he also put thoughts into the mind of Boaz. God does whatever he pleases. He wanted Elijah and

175

Elisha, not to mention Paul, to do certain things. He wanted them to think certain thoughts and make certain decisions. Whatever God wanted, he did. They did not choose God, independently; God chose them.

A story has recently gone around that an evangelist distributed bumper stickers, reading "I found him." Then some other people in the same city put on stickers that read, "He found me."

The long list of verses quoted here may seem tedious. It would be more so if all the supporting material, three to six times more extensive, were given. But even the small number quoted should apprise everyone of the pervasiveness of predestination in the Old Testament. And if Psalm 115:3 is not enough, note its repetition in Psalm 135:6, "Whatsoever the Lord pleased, that did he in heaven, and in earth, in the seas, and all deep places." God's control is not limited to the angels in heaven and the mollusks of the seas. It extends to the earth, where the human race forms the most important part.

Psalm 139:1-24 will complete the list from this longest of Old Testament books. This remarkable Psalm, which the Hugenots and Covenanters sang with deep devotion, extols in particular God's omniscience and omnipresence. There may be verses in the Bible which in a general way and by a universal proposition assert that God knows everything. Acts 15:18, "Known unto God are all his works," might be such a one. But this Psalm describes his knowledge of David. God knows David better than David knows himself (v. 6). The details are numerous; but of course twenty-four verses cannot list ten thousand. Nevertheless the idea is given that God knows David completely. Now, what is true of David here must be true of every human being. Did God know only David, and not Caesar, Charlemagne, and John Doe?

Note further what and how God knew David and every man. Verse 15 begins to speak of David's condition before he was born, when he was made in secret in the womb. All his

176

members were written down in God's book, like an accurate blueprint. Yet the translation is somewhat imperfect. Instead of the word *members*, the Hebrew says *days*, which then were continuously fashioned, before any of these days began. The RSV, which cannot be trusted, has *days* instead of members. The common German version reads, "und waren alle *Tage* auf dein Buch geschrieben, die noch werden sollten." Ostervald's French version also has *days*. This verse cannot properly be restricted to the number of days David was to live, without any reference to what he did in them. The Psalm has already specified his sitting down and his getting up. It explicitly mentions his thoughts in verse two. God knows *all* his ways, including every word of his tongue. These actions, words, and thoughts had been accurately written down in God's book before any of them took place. This is predestination. Every thought and deed had been determined from eternity. God does everything he pleases. He executes his blueprints meticulously. And David had no free will by which he could have made God's book a book of falsehoods.

Even the book of Proverbs, which consists mainly of ethical instructions, contains, though only a few, some very strong statements on predestination. In the Pinnock book Proverbs comes immediately after Genesis. There is nothing on Job and Psalms. Clearly this is not consistent with the method Dr. Clines laid down in his opening paragraph. Now, on Proverbs he says, "When it is a matter of how a man should live his life, Proverbs is saying *divine* [ital. his] predestination is not the point; what counts is how a *man* [ital. mine] is determining his own future . . . in the sense of human self-predestination it is central to the teaching of the book."

That the Proverbs are proverbs, instructing men what it is right to choose, cannot be contested. Nor is it relevant to the main matter. The main matter is whether predestination is divine or human. Is it man or is it God who predestines and

177

foreordains? Man indeed chooses—no Calvinist denies it; but the question is, Does God control the choice, or does man act independently? Let us examine Proverbs and see. Proverbs 16:1 reads, "The preparations of the heart in man, and the answer of the tongue is from the Lord." The King James margin gives "disposings" as an alternate for "preparations." This verse, rather clearly, is not restricted to the facts of conversion alone. It quite generally covers all the thoughts of one's heart and all the answers one gives to any question. In this God works, not merely by ordinary methods of persuasion or other means of uncertain power, but by omnipotent effectiveness. All the indirect material relative to God's sovereignty, passed over so briefly in the foregoing pages, gives the background for God's complete control of men's minds and thoughts. The verse in Proverbs continues by indicating that the words we speak, as well as the preparation of the heart, are from the Lord. That this is true, not only of devout Christians, but also of wicked kings, has been said before and will be said again.

In fact it is said again only three verses further on. Proverbs 16:4 states, "The Lord hath made all things for himself: yea, even the wicked for the day of evil." Is this not clear enough to force an Arminian to become a Calvinist or to reject Christianity altogether? Methinks it would, if the Arminian were rational. God made the wicked. Like a potter with indifferent clay, God made, of the same lump, vessels of dishonor as well as vessels of honor. This was part of his eternal plan, and every part of it contributes to the manifestation of his power and glory.

A moment ago reference was made to wicked kings. Proverbs 21:1 speaks of all kings, good and bad: "The king's heart is in the hand of the Lord . . . he turneth it withersoever he will." Surely no one can seriously maintain that this refers only to the one king who happened to be reigning when the verse was first written down. It applies to Pharaoh, to

178

Abimelech, and, as we shall see, to Cyrus, and to every other ruler. God turns their hearts withersoever he will. He caused Hitler's decision to invade Russia—much to Churchill's delight. He also caused Pontius Pilate to execute Christ. Had not God controlled this governor, Pilate might have listened to his wife's warning and so wrecked the whole divine plan of salvation. God turns the hearts and thoughts of rulers any way he pleases; and common citizens, subjects, or slaves are not a whit more independent or free. No one can choose otherwise than as God ordains.

It is instructive to note how the Pinnock book attempts to empty this verse of its significance. Dr. Clines writes, "Again, when we find . . . [Prov. 21:1], we do not have some doctrinaire assertion that a king never makes any decisions of his own and is only a puppet in God's hand. That would be contrary to the general outlook of Proverbs, though the proverb in isolation could doubtless mean that. Rather, what is taught here is that God, the world's governor, cannot be thwarted even by kings. . . ."

The Calvinist may take some wry comfort in the admission that the verse in isolation "could doubtless mean" what the Calvinist says it means. He can also approve of not taking it in isolation. Not only must it have its Proverbs context, but Proverbs as a whole should not be isolated from the rest of the Bible, especially not from Exodus through Psalms, from which the Pinnock author isolates it. As for his reference to puppets, one must note that the Bible does not refer to puppets; it speaks of a potter and clay. Incidentally, clay is more flexible and plastic than puppets.

The present study is not intended as a formal theological disquisition. Its aim is to present a fair sample of Old Testament material on the general subject of God's governance of "all his creatures and all their actions." Nevertheless, it is not illegitimate, even with such a restricted aim, to point out some of the ramifications. *The Freedom of the Will* (Erasmus) and *The Bondage of the Will* (Luther) have implications that permeate theology from beginning to end. An excellent volume on the subject is Loraine Boettner's *The Reformed Doctrine of Predestination,* published by the Presbyterian and Reformed Publishing Company. Topics which are immediately dependent on a view of predestination include the fall of man and his present sinful state, the doctrine of regeneration, the possibility of assurance and sanctification, and, most emphasized in Arminian objections, the question of moral responsibility.

In a more detailed and technical way all this includes theories of volition. Something on this matter can now provide an example of the theology involved, and also a break in the long list of biblical citations.

Predestination is a form of necessitarianism. There are of course other forms, neither Calvinistic nor even Christian. Atheistic mechanism with its behavioristic psychology is necessitarian. But if this were an argument against Calvinism, the Arminians would be convicted of Epicureanism, or at least of Romanism. Whether Professor William Cunningham was or was not a necessitarian, he defended the orthodoxy of Dr. Thomas Chalmers against the accusations of Sir William Hamilton. Augustus Toplady and Jonathan Edwards were also necessitarians.

Toplady devoted great energy to opposing John Wesley. Toplady wrote, "Arminianism has paved the way [to atheism] by despoiling the Divine Being, among other attributes, of his unlimited supremacy . . . of his invincible power, of his absolute independency. . . . Not to observe that the exemption of some things and events from the providence of God, by referring them to free-will, to contingency, and to chance . . . " (*Complete Works*, London, 1869, p. 278 col. 1).

In contrast with Calvinism the Arminian theory of the will may be called the theory of contingency. Or it may be described as the liberty of indifference: that is to say, no motives determine the will. It can choose the weaker motive over the stronger, or, what is more to the point, it can choose without any motive at all. This ability is frequently called the power of contrary choice. Given a set of antecedents, not only external but also internal, the will's decision could have been the reverse of what it was. A contingent event is one which may or may not happen. It is devoid of certainty, and therefore cannot be foreknown or predicted. Thus the doctrine of free will is a denial of omniscience.

One of the most common Arminian arguments against Calvinism is that necessitarianism destroys moral responsibility because the latter depends on freewill. Another article gave the Calvinistic defense of responsibility;[2] here the writer will only note that the indeterministic Epicureans, though not so immoral as frequently depicted, were less strict than the "fatalistic" Stoics; and that the Pharisees, though hypocrites, were more meticulous in their morality than the indeterministic Sadducees. Nor can one resist the temptation to contrast the Calvinists and the Jesuits.

These parenthetical paragraphs have been inserted at this point because the prophecy of Isaiah is such a major contribution to the main topic that it deserves whatever emphasis this break in the list of verses can provide.

Isaiah has some two dozen verses that bear rather directly on the doctrine of predestination. This estimate does not include complete paragraphs which, like Isaiah 6, describe in terms of grandeur the glorious and awful sovereignty of God.

However, two verses, verses nine and ten, from Isaiah 6, must be listed. "Go and tell this people, Hear ye . . . but understand not. . . . Make the heart of this people fat and make their ears heavy, and shut their eyes, lest they see with

---

[2]Determinism and Responsibility, *The Evangelical Quarterly,* Vol. IV, No. 1, 1932.

their eyes, and hear with their ears, and understand with their heart, and be healed." Perhaps at a later date God would convert them, and even in the interval, "until the cities be wasted," there might be a tenth who would worship God; but for the most part Isaiah was to preach so as to blind their eyes, close their ears, and cause them stupidly to misunderstand in their hearts. Consider: This is the same chapter in which Isaiah saw the Lord on his throne and his train filled the temple. Do verses nine and ten contradict verses one to four? Or is this how "the whole earth is full of his glory"?

The same idea, and possibly a part of the same situation, is repeated in Isaiah 19:14: "The Lord hath mingled a perverse spirit in the midst thereof; and they have caused Egypt to err in every work. . . ." The animosity toward the doctrine of predestination is largely, though perhaps not entirely, due to the idea that God causes evil and sin. One might even think that if indeed he did, the Scriptures would disguise, dilute, and hide the terrible truth. Quite the contrary, the Old Testament is full of it, and God's causation of good seems less frequently mentioned. This does not mean that the Old Testament is devoid of God's mercy and loving kindness. Such is frequent enough. The meaning is simply that the direct references to predestination seem to envisage evil more often than good. The New Testament reverses the proportion. But both Testaments explicitly and emphatically teach both.

Next, Isaiah 29:16 repeats the theme of the potter and the clay, and condemns anyone who complains. Incidentally, Pharaoh never complained.

"Comfort ye, comfort ye my people, saith your God. Speak comfortably" in tones that Handel beautifully approximated. Yet Isaiah 40:12-17 warns those who think they are something by reason of their free independence of God: "Who hath measured the waters in the hollow of his hand. . . . Who hath directed the Spirit of the Lord or, being his counsellor, hath taught him? With whom took he counsel, and who instructed

182

him. . . . Behold the nations are as a drop of a bucket, and are counted as the small dust of the balance. . . . All nations before him are as nothing. . . ."

That this rebukes the proud independence of free will is obvious; but there is another idea here also. Most Arminians—there are some consistent exceptions—admit that God is omniscient. Then when a Calvinist insists that God knows what a man will do at some future date, Arminians answer that knowledge does not imply control. Examples are given: standing on a promontory or a high tower, below which two roads meet at right angles, an observer sees two cars approaching the intersection at high speed. The observer knows they will collide, but it is not he who causes the collision.

Two mistakes ruin this illustration. The first mistake is that the observer does not really know. The collision might be probable; but just possibly one of the cars hits a boulder that has dropped from the cliff in a spot the observer cannot see. The other car continues unharmed. Man is not omniscient; God is. The second flaw in the illustration has at least a better notion of omniscience: even if God knows everything, they say, he does not cause the event in question. But if God knows a future event, the event is inevitable. If it were not inevitable, then God might "know" a future event that finally never takes place. But this is ignorance, not knowledge. If in 2000 B.C. God knew that Hitler would invade Russia, or that I should get a hair cut on October 3 at 2:20 P.M., the event would be inevitable. Now, if God did not determine it, who did? The event was certain back in 2000 B. C. If God did not make it certain, there must be, beside God, another power that fixes at least some future events. That these events will occur, God discovers empirically by looking into the future and seeing what events his rival decided to cause.

Such a view is utterly anti-scriptural. "Who hath directed the Spirit of the Lord, or being his counsellor hath taught him? . . . Who instructed him . . . and taught him knowledge?"

183

Oh, no one taught him, someone may say. He found it out by himself. He just examined how his created universe ran itself, and with the sagacity of Sir Isaac Newton discovered what would happen in the future. No one taught Newton. But if Newton had created the planets and carefully arranged their mechanism so that they would revolve in elliptical orbits, and if he had the omnipotence to create a perfect mechanism, he would not have had to look into the future and discover how they were moving. He would have known how they were moving because he had made them that way. Now, God is not only a great astronomer; he is also an omnipotent and therefore omniscient psychologist.

If the theme of God's foreordination of evil events seems to have been overemphasized in the foregoing—though it is the biblical emphasis and not an invention of the present writer—Isaiah 43:7 says that God created, and therefore foreordained, for his own glory, those who bear his name. Who dares to say that not even God can help them? Indeed they come to him willingly; but it is God who set his name on them and made them willing. Verse 10 continues, "Ye are my witnesses, saith the Lord, and my servants whom I have chosen that ye may believe me and understand that I am he. Before me there was no other god formed [who determined events for me to discover empirically], neither shall there be after me." God chose his servants for a purpose, and God's purposes cannot fail. Isaiah then repeats it: "This people have I formed for myself: they shall show forth my praise." Can these people, by an alleged free, undetermined will, refuse? By no means: "they *shall* show forth my praise" (43:21).

Isaiah 45 is an overpowering assertion of God's sovereignty. It begins with Cyrus, the Lord's annointed, and a statement of what God will do by him and for him. Then comes what is probably the most exalted statement in the Bible about the sovereignty of God. It is utterly destructive of Arminianism. The later verses, clear in themselves, are not to be ignored; but the middle section beggars praise. Verse five is only a reminder of the whole: "I am the Lord, and there is none else, there is no God beside me. I girded thee, though thou hast not known me."

It is a shame to interrupt even an incomplete quotation, but the present task is to call attention to its meaning. God girded Cyrus, though Cyrus did not know it. One must not suppose, when God girds, guides, and controls someone, that the person is aware of it. Even regeneration, as the Puritans pointed out, is not a conscious experience; much less God's control of Pharaoh, Absalom, or Cyrus. Their knowledge comes later, if at all. Then the text continues: "I am the Lord, and there is none else. I form the light and create darkness; I make peace and create evil. I the Lord do all these things."

The two theses most unacceptable to the Arminians are that God is the cause of sin and that God is the cause of salvation. In both cases the Arminians look to free will. Man is the first cause of his sin, and, still independent of God, man is the first cause of his conversion. Isaiah in this verse makes Arminianism biblically impossible.

The Scofield Bible is a good example of how Arminians try to escape from the plain meaning of the verse. Scofield says, "Heb. ra, translated 'sorrow,' 'wretchedness,' 'adversity,' 'afflictions,' 'calamities,' but never translated *sin*. God created evil only in the sense that he made sorrow, wretchedness, etc., to be the sure fruits of sin."

Now the most remarkable point about Scofield's note is that he told the truth when he said, "*ra* . . . [is] never translated sin." How could he have made such a statement, knowing it was true? The only answer is that he must have examined every instance of *ra* in the Hebrew text and then he must have determined that in no case did King James translate it sin. And this is absolutely true. But if he compared every instance of *ra* with its translation in every case, he could not have failed to note that *ra* in Genesis 6:5 and in a number of other places is translated *wickedness*. In fact *ra* is translated *wickedness* some fifty times. Scofield could not have failed to notice this; so he says with just truth, *ra* is never translated sin. Since Scofield favors the word *evil*, a partial list of verses in which this translation occurs will be given; and second there will be a partial list where *wicked* or *wickedness* is used.

Going through the Bible, Scofield must have read as far as Genesis 2:9, 17; 3:5, 22; 6:5; 8:21; 44:4; 48:16; 50:15, 17, 20. "The knowledge of good and *evil*" is not simply a knowledge of sorrow or calamity; it is primarily a knowledge of disobedience and sin. Similarly Genesis 3:5, 22 refers as much to sin as to its punishment. In fact Genesis 3:22 hardly refers to punishment at all. True, Adam was banished from the garden; but the word *evil* in the verse refers to his disobedience and sin.

Whatever lame excuse can be given for excluding sin and retaining only punishment in the previous four verses, Genesis 6:5 is clearly and indisputably a reference to sin. God did not see "adversity" or "afflictions"; he saw sinful thoughts. *Ra*, in this verse at any rate, means sin. The same is true of Genesis 8:21. In fact sin and its punishment are separated here. God will not again curse or smite, as he had just done, for man's heart is evil. The flood was a punishment, but the evil was the sinful heart of man.

Toward the end of Genesis *ra* refers to an alleged theft, many sins from which the Angel had redeemed Jacob, and three times the brothers' sin against Joseph. In 50:17 again the sin is easily distinguishable from the feared punishment.

Is it necessary to plod through all the Old Testament to show that *ra* often means sin as distinct from its punishment? It should not be necessary; but to show the pervasiveness of the doctrine and the perverseness of Arminianism, something from II Chronicles will be listed: 22:4; 29:6; 33:2, 6; 36:5, 9, 12. Ahab did *evil* in the sight of the Lord. Our fathers have trespassed and done evil in the eyes of the Lord. Manasseh

186

did evil in the sight of the Lord. He wrought much evil in the sight of the Lord. Jehoiakim did evil in the sight of the Lord. He did evil in the sight of the Lord.

Evil, *ra*, is not once *translated* sin. Very strange, but true.

Then there are Isaiah 56:2; 57:1; 59:7, 15; 65:12; 66:4. All instances of *ra*, or *evil*.

Now, if Scofield knew that *ra* was never translated *sin*, he must have known that it was often translated *wickedness*. *Wickedness* or *wicked*, as the translation of *ra* occurs in Genesis 6:5; 13:13; 38:7; 39:9. Also in Deuteronomy 13:11 and 17:2. Also in I Samuel 30:22 and II Samuel 3:39. I Kings 2:44; Nehemiah 9:35; Esther 7:6, 9, 25. And Proverbs 21:12; 26:23, 26. Nor are these the only instances.

Scofield told the literal truth when he said it is never translated *sin*. But nothing could be more false than his statement, "God created evil *only* in the sense that he made sorrow, wretchedness, etc., to be the sure fruits of sin."

The scriptural meaning of the word *ra*, has now been abundantly made clear. But there is another point too. If *ra* means simply external calamities, then the word *peace*, which God also creates, can mean only military peace. The phrases are parallel. But this interpretation reduces the verse, or this part of the verse, to triviality. Even verse one can hardly be restricted to purely political matters. Verse three speaks of treasures of darkness, hidden riches, and the knowledge of God. Jacob my servant and Israel my elect are not phrases to be restricted to politics and economics. Verse 6 speaks of the extension of the knowledge of God throughout the world. Then comes "I make peace and create evil." Merely military peace? Not peace with God? The next verse speaks of righteousness dropping down from heaven, not like dew, but like pouring rain. Bring forth salvation, let righteousness spring up together. I the Lord have created it.

O, Arminian, Arminian, thou that distortest the prophets and misinterpretest them that are sent unto thee; how often have I told your children the plain truth . . . and ye would not let them understand!

There is still more in this chapter from Isaiah. Once again we find the potter and the clay. It indicates that God is not responsible to man. Woe to the man who complains that God has made him or anyone else a vessel of dishonor. The clay has no "rights" against the potter. Nor does it have any free will to decide what sort of a bowl or jug it shall be.

The dark, unpleasant side of the doctrine, precisely because it is unpleasant, is offensive to human pride. But the two sides are sides of the same coin. God is sovereign in mercy also. After stressing God's creative power in 45:12, Isaiah continues, "I have raised him [Cyrus] up in righteousness and I will direct all his ways." This applies to all that Cyrus did. Of course, Isaiah who made the prediction and the devout Jews who fulfilled it were chiefly interested in Cyrus' treatment of them; but God directed Cyrus in all the details of his empire and in all the details of his private life.

What the Bible affirms so clearly, Dr. Clines denies. On page 122 he writes, "It cannot be shown that the prophets believed in a fixed plan that extended from the beginning to the end of world history. . . . The prophetic predictions . . . do not amount to a claim that all the events of history move toward a divine goal. They are rather an assertion that within history God is working his purposes out." Now, Isaiah 45:13 does not mention *all* the actions of the judges or the later kings of Judah and Israel. Nonetheless, pointedly and explicitly, it mentions all the ways of Cyrus. But, then, Dr. Clines, in his "Predestination in the Old Testament" not only skips over Judges and Kings, he has no section on Isaiah either. Admittedly there are two, or perhaps three, verses quoted; and there are four or five verses referred to by number; but the great amount of decisive material, as given here, Dr. Clines omits. The Calvinist does not want to "fail to see the whole range of biblical revelation on the subject" (p. 110).

188

The next chapter is equally forceful. Isaiah 46:10, 11 reads, "Declaring the end from the beginning . . . things that are not yet done, saying, My counsel shall stand and I will do all my pleasure. . . . I have spoken it, I will also bring it to pass; I have proposed it, I will also do it."

From the beginning God purposed to use Cyrus, and he did so. God determined that Daniel should do this and that, and God brought it to pass. God predicted that one of Christ's disciples should betray him, and God executed his eternal decree in Judas. God purposed to regenerate Peter, John, and Paul. It also pleased God that Hank Aaron should hit more home runs than Babe Ruth, and the pitcher could not have done better nor the batter worse. What God purposes, he does. Let no one raise his eyebrows at the mention of Hank Aaron. If this chapter covered the New Testament, it would be clear that God determined the number of hairs on Hank Aaron's head.

Few chapters in the Bible are as sublime as Isaiah 53. It begins with a prediction of the Messiah's death. This prediction and every other prediction presupposes that God can and does control every factor bearing on the result. This particular prediction may not bear so directly on the choice of some Chinese peasant who lived in A.D. 800; but it certainly bears on Annas, Caiaphas, the soldier who pierced Jesus' side, and more directly on Joseph of Arimathaea.

Arminians are likely to say that if Caiaphas in his freedom had not willed to prosecute, some other high priest would have done so. But if the other priest had had free will too, maybe he would have chosen the twentieth of Nisan rather than the fourteenth. And if the soldiers had had free will, they might have broken Jesus' legs. That they could not have chosen so to do is guaranteed by Exodus 12:46 and Numbers 9:12.

There is more. When it pleased the Lord to bruise him, and the Lord does all his pleasure, the Messiah saw his seed, the "many" whom John calls his people; he saw the travail of his soul, and was satisfied. Now, if Jesus on the cross had in-

189

tended to save the wicked inhabitants of Sodom and Gomorrah, already condemned in hell, his intentions would have been defeated and he would not have been satisfied. Jesus did not intend to save everybody. He intended to save his seed.

The Arminians usually try to escape the force of this argument by replying that Jesus never intended to save anybody. He only intended to make salvation possible for everybody. Calvinists insist that Christ provided salvation, actual salvation, for those whom the Father gave him. Actual salvation, not just a chance of salvation. As an advertising gimmick the supermarket may offer everybody a chance on fifty pounds of sugar. But a chance is not sugar. That Christ did not intend to give actual salvation to anyone is amply refuted by God's choice of Abraham. Surely Christ intended to apply his merits to the friends of God. The Lamb that was slain from the foundation of the world did not intend to save those whose names were not written in the book of life from the foundation of the world (Rev. 13:8 and 17:8), but he surely intended to save the people his Father had given him.

This main idea is pointedly expressed again in Isaiah 55:11. "So shall my word be that goeth forth out of my mouth. It shall not return unto me void, but it shall accomplish that which I please, and it shall prosper in the thing whereto I sent it." The immediate example of this is the next verse: "For ye shall go out with joy and be led forth with peace. . . ."

There are indeed verses on reprobation, like Isaiah 45:7; but in these two chapters we see the free grace that prevents the tragedies of free will. God's word accomplishes its intention. Return first to Isaiah 49, which we just passed over in silence.

"Listen . . . ye people. . . . The Lord hath called me from the womb. . . . He hath made my mouth like a sharp sword . . . and said unto me, Thou art my servant, O Israel, in whom I will be glorified. . . . And now, saith the Lord that formed me from the womb to be his servant, . . . though Israel be not gathered, yet I shall be glorious in the eyes of the Lord. . . .

190

And he said, Is it a light thing that thou shouldst be my servant . . . I will also give thee for a light to the Gentiles. . . ." And the man replied, Oh, no! I will not be thy servant, I will not be a light unto the Gentiles, and you cannot make me, for I have free will.

Fortunately these last two lines have poor textual attestation.

The point is that when God says he will do something, and by the man he chooses, whether Cyrus or Judas, the agent has no free will to resist. He is clay and the Potter molded him for his purpose. Prophecy is an important testimony to predestination. Isaiah 60 predicts: "The Lord shall arise upon thee . . . the Gentiles shall come to thy light. . . . They shall show forth the praises of the Lord. . . . The sons of strangers shall build up thy walls, . . . for in my wrath I smote thee, but in my favor have I had mercy on thee. . . . The glory of Lebanon shall come to thee. . . The sons also of them that afflicted thee shall come bending unto thee . . . and they shall call thee The City of the Lord . . . Thou shalt know that I am the Lord. . . . Thou shalt call thy walls Salvation and thy gates Praise. The sun shall be no more thy light . . . but the Lord shall be unto thee an everlasting light, and thy God thy glory. . . . Thy people also shall be all righteousness."

Our opponents will try to dismiss all this as irrelevant. These verses, they will say, refer to large groups of people, and God will also find someone to do what he foretells: if one person does not choose him freely, another will. Among a billion people, someone will also seek the Lord and do his will.

But Psalm 14:1-3 has already asserted the contradictory: "There is none that doeth good." The Lord looked down from heaven—as the Arminians say he must in order to learn what independent beings are up to—to see if there were any that did understand and seek God. [But, no]; "There are all gone aside . . . there is none that doeth good, no not one." Later Ezekiel will picture them as a valley of dry bones.

Now, note that in Isaiah 60:19-21 the important thing is not political power and external prestige. It says, the people shall be righteous. This is predestination in Christ to eternal life. This is "the work of my hands that I may be glorified." No doubt the Lord uses means in the process of sanctification; but the means are effective, or else he could not do all his pleasure and the Messiah would not be satisfied.

Let it also be noted that while there are great historical and social movements of masses of people, these mass movements are performed by individuals choosing that line of action. God may bless an age with a Great Awakening. But, for this, one individual after another must be individually awakened from his sinful slumber of death.

Isaiah 64:8 will be the last of the list from this great Old Testament book. No doubt some verses from the final two chapters could be added. Isaiah 65:9 makes a prediction; 65:15 speaks of those whom God has chosen; 65:22 refers to God's elect. Chapter 66 begins with an expression of God's sovereignty. "The heaven is my throne and the earth is my footstool." Then there comes a denunciation of those who have "chosen their own ways"; to which is added, "I will choose their delusions." Here again is a case of God's controlling a man's mind. The man must think what God makes him think, even when these thoughts are delusions. Similarly when the thoughts are good thoughts: "Shall I bring to the birth and not cause to bring forth?" This is not literal physical birth, but "Rejoice . . . that ye may suck and be satisfied with the breasts of her consolations . . . and be delighted with the abundance of her glory . . . and they shall declare my glory to the Gentiles."

After such passages as this, who can limit God's power or his effective activity?

But the last verse to be quoted will be Isaiah 64:8. It is the same as we heard before. Here it is expressed, not as God's declaration, but as man's ascription of praise to God. "But

192

now, O Lord, thou art our father; we are the clay, and thou art our potter, and we all are the work of thy hand."

> Have thine own way, Lord
> Have thine own way.
> Hold o'er my being
> Absolute sway.

By this time the Arminians, if they could endure to read this far, will be loudly complaining that the writer has selected all the Calvinistic verses and none of the Arminian verses. Well, the writer had not found any Arminian verses. However there are some verses that Arminians use, and Jeremiah 4:4 could be one of them. It is a quotation from or repetition of Deuteronomy 10:4. "Circumcise yourselves to the Lord, and take away the foreskins of your heart." Isaiah 1:16, 17 is essentially similar: "Wash you and make you clean; put away the evil of your doings from before mine eyes. . . ." Do not these verses affirm that an evil doer can change his heart, cleanse and regenerate himself?

Since it is possible, if all the indirect, supportive material be omitted, to treat the book of Jeremiah more briefly than Isaiah, a little lengthier reply to the objection can be made. However, three other verses help. Jeremiah 17:9 says "The heart is deceitful above all things and desperately wicked." Such a heart neither could, nor could want to cleanse itself. Jeremiah 18:6, for the thousandth time, repeats the potter and the clay. Jeremiah 32:17 asserts omnipotence: "Ah, Lord God, behold thou hast made the heaven and the earth . . . there is nothing too hard for thee," not even the heart of man. But what about "Circumcise the foreskins of your heart"?

This is a command, and as such it seems to imply that a man can obey or disobey as he chooses. Otherwise, he would not be responsible, for as Pope Immanuel Kant said, Ability limits responsibility, or, if I ought, I can. Conversely, if circumcision of the heart or the washing of regeneration were wrought only by the irresistible grace of God, and man were purely passive therein, these commands to wicked men are useless and indeed hypocritical.

In answer to this Arminian argument, the first thing to insist upon is that men are filthy and need to be washed; but more than this, they are so filthy that they cannot clean themselves, either by Old Testament ceremonial ablutions or by any New Testament ordinance. Proverbs 20:9 asks the rhetorical question, "Who can say, I have made my heart clean?" The cleansing of the heart is God's work, for it is God who creates a clean heart within and washes sinners thoroughly from their iniquities (Ps. 51:2, 10). Recall also Ezekiel 36:25, "Then will I sprinkle clean water upon you, and ye shall be clean; from all your filthiness and from all your idols will I cleanse you."

At this point the nonplused Arminians reply, But if this is the work of God alone, and man does not help in it at all, then of what use are these commands? Since they must be of some use, man must be able at least to help in cleansing himself.

This reply, however, fails because it is based on a logical fallacy. It supposes that since the command cannot have the use the Arminians want it to have, it can have no use at all. Since the Scripture very clearly says that man cannot cleanse himself at all, one must see what use the Scripture assigns to such commands. This is not hard to do. Romans 3:20 says, "By the law is the knowledge of sin." Commands are given, not because any man can obey them, but in order to convince man that he is a sinner. Let him try to obey and he will find he cannot. When a man discovers this, he will be more willing to see the need of divine grace. Proverbs 30:12 mentions "a generation that are pure in their own eyes, and yet is not washed from their filthiness." The commands under discussion are intended to convince some sinners that they are not clean and that they cannot wash themselves. Hence the commands are not in vain, nor do they contradict the gospel of grace.

Note further in connection with this verse that the figurative expression of circumcising the heart very probably does not refer to regeneration or conversion. When God commanded Abraham to circumcise Isaac, Abraham was already a sincere worshiper of God. So too was Isaac. Instead of this verse having to do with regeneration, it more probably indicates some works subsequent to regeneration. It means that the people now being regenerate should immediately begin to mortify the deeds of the flesh and strive toward righteousness. This interpretation would empty the verse of all Arminian value.

However, it is possible that the verse could refer to regeneration. Even so, it has no Arminian value. We read in the New Testament about the circumcision of the heart, in the Spirit and not in the letter, whose praise is of God, not of men (Rom. 2:29). Note that literal circumcision was performed by a man, and insofar as it was done in obedience to God, the man was worthy of a measure of commendation: the Lord could say, Well done, thou good and faithful servant. But this circumcision is not performed by a man. It is a circumcision made without hands (Col. 2:11). Even a circumcision of the flesh, administered to infants, expresses the passivity of the recipient. If this is true of the type and Old Testament shadow, it must be much more true of the New Testament reality. Incidentally, the translation, "Circumcise yourselves" could be improved to "Be ye circumcised." The verb here and in the Septuagint is passive. Even the Latin Vulgate has the passive voice.

As an appendix to Jeremiah, Lamentation 3:37-38 declares, "Who is he that saith, and it cometh to pass, when the Lord commandeth it not? Out of the mouth of the most High, proceedeth not [both] good and evil?" Note that neither Cyrus, Alexander the Great, Pontius Pilate, nor Martin Luther could bring anything to pass unless God commanded it. For the

195

who of the verse includes Luther and the Pope as well as Pilate. Pilate could give no order to his soldiers unless it was God's command. So, when Luther said, "Here I stand," he spoke what God decreed he should speak.

Ezekiel in addition to all the indirect material, which is always present when the Scripture speaks of the majesty of God, has three pointed assertions of God's control over the spiritual condition of men. The first of these is Ezekiel 11:19, which says, "I will give them one heart, and I will put a new spirit within you; and I will take the stony heart out of their flesh, and will give them a heart of flesh."

Here we have a divine heart transplant. Obviously a patient cannot perform a heart transplant on himself. There must be a surgeon. In this case God is the surgeon. Not only so, but in this case the patient did not want a heart transplant. He was quite satisfied with his stony heart. He was at enmity with God and was entirely uncooperative. There is none that seeketh God, no not one. The patient with his evil mind would have resisted the operation, if he could have done so. But God is irresistible. When God says, I will remove your present heart and give you another, he does what he says he will. No one can stop him. When it says that God will put a new spirit within them, it means that God will cause them to think other thoughts. They will then decide to "take away all the detestable things thereof and all the abominations." Recall that God had sent the Israelites into captivity because of their detestable practices and abominations. Now, God may have used and no doubt did use the rigors of exile to change their minds. God does not disdain to use means. He chooses and controls both the means and the people's reaction so as to accomplish his aim. His aim is not only a change of geography, but a change of mind.

The predestination or foreordination of what people think, as well as what they do, is even more strongly stated in Ezekiel 36:25-27. "Then will I sprinkle clean water upon you,

196

and ye shall be clean: from all your filthiness, and from all your idols, will I cleanse you. A new heart also will I give you, and a new spirit will I put within you: and I will take away the stony heart out of your flesh, and I will give you an heart of flesh. And I will put my spirit within you, and cause you to walk in my statutes, and ye shall keep my judgments, and do them."

The first of these verses states that God will cleanse these people. He will cleanse them from all their filthiness. What God says he will do, he does. God's grace is irresistible. No man can by any act of will prevent God from cleansing him, regenerating him, or giving him a new heart and mind. This last is what the next verse says, repeating Ezekiel 11:19. Permit a New Testament corroboration. John 1:13, with some paraphrasing, says, The sons of God are born as sons of God, not by reason of their ancestral blood, for God can of these stones raise up children to Abraham; nor by any volition of any unregenerate human nature, for no one seeks God; nor by any individual act of will at all. A man is born a son only by the will of God. John and Ezekiel agree. God chooses whom he will cleanse and whom he will regenerate, and he accomplishes all his intent and pleasure.

The following verse, Ezekiel 36:27, goes a step further. Not only does God surgically transplant a heart, but he sees to it that the new heart functions in a satisfactory manner; for with the heart he also implants his Spirit and thus causes his patients to walk according to the Ten Commandments. That is to say, he so controls the volitions of his newly born sons that they walk in his statutes. Thus sanctification is also inevitable and irresistible. There is, to be sure, a difference in method, though not in effectiveness. In regeneration man's will has no part whatever; in sanctification God causes the new heart, mind, and will to function properly—at least in increasing degree of perfection. God will cause them to remember their old evil ways and to loathe themselves because of

197

their earlier iniquities and abominations. Then in further verses God will cause them to do some other things.

In this instance the Hebrew not only has the verb in the causative Hiphil form, but also adds the verb *make*. The result is a sort of double causation or added emphasis to the causative idea.

As for translations, not only does the RSV retain the causative force of the verb, but even the Roman Catholic *Jerusalem Bible*, says, "je *ferai* que vous marchiez selon mes lois." The footnote itself, in which perhaps the translators did not quite realize what they were saying, states, "Plus mysterieusement, l'Esprit sera, pour chacun, principe de renouvellement interieur, qui le rendra apte a observer fidelement la Loi divine." English: "I will make you walk according to my laws; [and] more mysteriously, the Spirit will be, for each one, the principle of internal renewal, who will render each one apt to observe the divine Law faithfully."

Perhaps the most powerful and certainly the most picturesque assertion of grace unconditional and irresistible comes in the next chapter. It is Ezekiel's vision of a "valley which was full of dry bones. . . . There were very many in the open valley; and lo, they were very dry." Then God asked Ezekiel, "Can these bones live?" Too humble or too awed at the majesty and omnipotence of God to give the obvious answer, No, Ezekiel replied, "O Lord God, Thou knowest." Then God said, "Prophesy . . . unto them, O ye dry bones, hear the word of the Lord." Of course the dry bones could no more hear Ezekiel than Lazarus could hear Christ. "Thus saith the Lord God," Ezekiel began, addressing the dry bones. Thus saith the Lord, "I will cause breath to enter into you and ye shall live; and I will lay sinews upon you, and will bring up flesh upon you. . . . And as I prophesied, . . . behold, there was a shaking and . . . lo the sinews and the flesh came up upon them . . . but there was no breath in them. Then said he unto me, Prophesy unto the wind . . . and the breath came into them, and they lived." An explanation follows: "These bones are the whole house of Israel, . . . I will open your graves and cause you to come up out of your graves . . . and shall put my Spirit in you and ye shall live . . . I the Lord have spoken it and performed it, saith the Lord."

In this passage every one of the five points of Calvinism fulfills its function; and as the list of Old Testament passages approaches its end, this is an excellent opportunity to tie the several doctrines together.

The first is the doctrine of total depravity. The unregenerate man is not sick, so as to drag himself to the pharmacy and buy some medicine; he is dead in sin. He is a heap of dry, very dry bones. He "is not able by his own strength to convert himself or to prepare himself thereunto" (*Westminster Confession*, IX 3). It is hard to think of any better illustration of total inability than a picture of bones dry in the desert. Dry bones cannot think or will. If they are to live, it must be by the omnipotent, unconditional grace of God.

It must be unconditional, for God finds no motivation in them to move him to action. There is no foreseen faith. Dead bones cannot believe or exercise any life-function whatever. Faith is a gift of God; he gives it to them whom he chooses, not on the condition that they already have some merit of their own, but unconditionally.

God does not choose everyone. The redemption he provides is limited to a certain number. Now, God may have chosen every one of those dry bones in that one valley. They may all be saved; but not all individuals who ever lived, or even who lived in Ezekiel's day, are saved. God always does what he intends; he never intended to save the Sodomites; therefore God's intention is limited. Those whom he chose, he gave to Christ, named Jesus, for he was to save his people from their sins.

The fourth of the five points Arminius attacked is irresistible grace. God said, "I will cause breath to enter into you, and ye shall live. And I will lay sinews upon you . . . and ye shall know that I am the Lord." When these dry bones were made alive, and because of this, they knew that God was the Lord. If they could have done the impossible, and made themselves alive, they might have had doubts. But because they later recognized that they could not have given themselves life, because they then knew that God was omnipotent and irresistible, they then knew who and what he was. Could the dry bones, by their own free will, have frustrated God's intention to save them? Does not God do whatever he pleases? Does he not fulfill his promises? Here his promises are: "Behold, O my people, I will open your graves and cause you to come up out of your graves . . . [I] shall put my Spirit in you and ye shall live. . . . I the Lord have spoken it and performed it." God's grace is irresistible. He does what he says he will do.

The fifth and final point is the perseverance of the saints. The Arminians hold that regeneration cannot assure us of entering heaven because our free will may someday negate our new birth. Then if we are to arrive in glory, we shall have to be regenerated a second, third, and fourth time. But until we are dead, we can have no assurance, for God cannot control and determine a free will. All this is utterly contrary to what Ezekiel says. Verses 15-20 promise that God will reunite Israel and Judah. He will bring them back to their land, with one king, namely King David. But note further. Verses 15-20 might be dismissed as merely political dealings with masses, and not with individual salvation. However, the Lord continues, "Neither shall they defile themselves any-more . . . but I will save them from all their dwelling places wherein they have sinned and will cleanse them . . . they shall also walk in my judgments and observe my statutes and do them . . . they and their children's children forever, and my servant David shall be their prince forever . . . an everlasting covenant . . . my sanctuary shall be in the midst of them forevermore."

Who is this David who shall be prince and king forevermore? Surely no one who returned from the Babylonian captivity or contributed to the temporary success of the Maccabees. No, this is a prediction of heavenly glory. The individuals whom God made alive out of dry bones and breathed into them his own Spirit, and whom he predetermined to observe his statutes and do them, these individuals are assured of their everlasting felicity. They cannot possibly fall from grace, but "shall certainly persevere therein to the end and be eternally saved" (*Westminster Confession*, XVII, 1). Otherwise grace, conditional grace, is no more grace.

This chapter in Ezekiel can easily be said to be the culmination of the Old Testament's teaching on predestination or foreordination. The TULIP is there in all its beauteous glory.

Before ending this study with a verse or two from Daniel and Zechariah, certain so-called Arminian verses in Ezekiel ought to be discussed. The reason is that Calvinists ought not to ignore such verses as Clines has ignored nearly everything the present article has brought to light. Whether the Arminians might prefer discussions of other verses, Ezekiel, chapters 18 and 33, are surely fair choices. The opponents cannot sustain an accusation against us of dodging a crucial passage.

To recall the passage to mind without quoting the whole chapter, Ezekiel 18 says, "The fathers have eaten sour grapes, and the children's teeth are set on edge . . . ye shall not have occasion any more to use this proverb . . . the soul that sinneth, it shall die. . . . Have I any pleasure at all that the wicked should die . . . and not that he should return from his ways and live?"

If the Calvinist takes wry pleasure in the Arminian's admission that Proverbs 21:1, taken in isolation, could mean what the Calvinist says it means, let us grant the Arminian his wry pleasure that Ezekiel 18:25, 32 could in isolation mean what the Arminian says. But neither of us wants to take his opponent's verse in isolation. There is a difference, however; whereas the Pinnock author examines only the context in Proverbs, and does not get even that much right, the Calvinist will not only examine all of Ezekiel, but all Exodus through Psalms, Isaiah, and the New Testament as well. To initiate such an examination, the reader should note that the verses omitted from the memory-jogging quotation above will affect the interpretation of the verse in question.

Now, Ezekiel 18 presents several difficulties. Verses 2, 4, and 20 could in isolation be taken as contradictory of Romans 5:12-21. The latter teaches that every man is guilty of Adam's first sin, immediately imputed. Ezekiel seems to deny this. This is not the place to discuss immediate imputation: the point is mentioned solely to show that Ezekiel 18 contains more than one difficulty.

Another difficulty, one that occurs in several books of the Bible, including Romans 2:10, 14, 25, occurs in Ezekiel 18:19, 21, 22, 27, 28, 31. These verses, in both books, sound as if some men could merit God's justification on the basis of their own works of righteousness. But the context in Romans and Galatians and elsewhere teaches justification by faith alone. Now, if these contexts so completely alter the superficial meaning of the verses in question, one must be prepared to alter the Arminian interpretation of verses 23 and 32.

As for the context of this chapter, several chapters in Ezekiel have already been discussed. There was the divine heart transplant of Ezekiel 11:19. This theme was extended in Ezekiel 36:25-27. Then there is the tremendous scene in Ezekiel 37. All this clear-cut Calvinism requires Ezekiel 18 to be interpreted within the same system of thought. Similarly the wider context from Genesis to Revelation.

But now to chapter 18 itself. Verse 31 says, "Make you a new heart." Does this mean that God does not make and implant the new heart? We have seen that such cannot be the case.

Next, there is the apparently innocuous form of address in the same verse: "O house of Israel." At this point one must note that Paul addresses "all that be in Rome"; "the church of God which is at Corinth"; "the church of Galatia," without any added reference to saints as in the first two books; then "unto the church of the Thessalonians which is in God the Father"; similarly II Thessalonians. While now the Arminian may disallow Romans and Corinthians, it is clear that Paul addresses the other two churches without any phrase that might indicate he is addressing only a part of their membership. He treats the congregations on the basis of their public profession, even though there may be several non-Christians among them.

Similarly in Ezekiel, the prophet addresses the house of Israel. Surely Ezekiel knew that "he is not a Jew which is one outwardly," and that "they are not all Israel which are of Israel."

Therefore the contiguous verse in Ezekiel, the context of the book as a whole, and the references in the New Testament indicate that God has no pleasure in the death of Israel. His warnings in this chapter are designed as an effective means of preventing their death, the Israel of God, and of avoiding a humanly contemplated frustration of God's original decree and choice.

Ezekiel 33 contains similar statements, which must be given the same interpretation. No doubt there are other so-called Arminian verses. Here the sample from Ezekiel 18 is sufficient to refute any Arminian accusation of ignoring their contentions. Especially any gentleman who skims so lightly over the Old Testament doctrine of predestination is precluded from making such an accusation.

Daniel 4:35 says, "I praised and honored him . . . whose dominion is an everlasting dominion . . . and all the inhabitants of the earth are reputed as nothing; and he doeth according to his will in the army of heaven and among the inhabitants of the earth; and none can stay his hand, or say unto him, What doest thou?" None can stay his hand, either in reprobation or redemption. No will is free and independent of God; but God does his will everywhere and always. God could have changed Nebuchadnezzar's mind and will instantaneously, as he did Paul's; but he usually works more gradually and in this instance took seven years.

Daniel 11:36 once again declares that what a man thinks and wills has been determined by God. The verse is a prediction that a king shall choose to do evil. Of course the king chooses; he exerts his will; he makes a decision. Calvinists do not deny that man exercises volition. The point is that the volition is predetermined, because: "the king shall do according to his will, and he shall exalt himself . . . and shall speak marvellous things against the God of gods . . . for that that is determined shall be done." God has predetermined or foreordained what this king should think, will, and do. And he did it.

The final Old Testament reference is Zechariah 12:10, which says, "And I will pour upon the house of David . . . the spirit of grace . . . and they shall" look and mourn. The important point is not what things they shall do, but that they do them under the control of the spirit of grace. The following chapter continues the predictions. One is that if a son prophesies falsely, his parents will put him to death. This surely is against natural impulse and requires the superintendence of God.

In conclusion, not only is predestination mentioned in the Old Testament, it is pervasive and emphatic. Seventy-five passages or more, some not just a verse but a whole chapter, have been quoted in full or in part. A tremendous amount of indirect evidence, of background material, has not been referred to at all. Predestination, unconditional election, sovereign grace, and reprobation also, are pervasive doctrines. No wonder the Westminster Confession makes the eternal decree the third most important of all biblical doctrines.

Soli gloria Deo.

INDEX OF SCRIPTURE

Genesis
1:1-25—42
1:1—7, 8, 152, 153-55, 173
1:18, 21, 25, 31—42
1:27—8
2—155
2:1—7
2:7—8, 9
2:9—186
2:16-17—155-56
2:17—88, 186
3:5, 22—186
4:19-24—42
6:5—12, 88, 172, 185-86, 187
6:17—9
7:15—9
8:21—186
12:1ff.—156
12:7—156
13:13—187
15:1—156
15:4-5—156
15:5—37
15:13—156
15:14—48
17:1—17, 156, 157
17:6—48
18:14—128
20:3-6—157

21:33—38
28:3—17, 157
31:1—29
38:7—187
39:9—187
44:4—186
48:16—186
49:6—71
50:15, 17, 20—186
50:20—44, 158

Exodus
3:19—159
4:21—54, 159, 160
6:3—17, 163
7:3, 13—54, 159, 160
7:14, 22—54, 160
7:22—160
8:15, 32—55, 160
8:19—54, 160
9:7, 35—54, 160
9:12—54, 160
9:16—30, 161
9:32—160
9:34—55
10:1, 20, 27—54, 160
11:10—54, 160
12:36—59
12:46—189

207

14:4, 8—54, 160
14:17—54, 160
33:19—80

Numbers
9:12—189
21:5—29
24:4, 16—163

Deuteronomy
2:30—53, 55, 161-62
5:29—130, 131, 140
10:4—135, 193
10:17—162
13:11—187
17:2—187
30:6—136, 162
30:19—131
31:20-21—44
33:16—72

Joshua
17:15, 18—15

Judges
2:7, 10-12—145

Ruth
1:20-21—17, 163

I Samuel
2:3—36, 163
2:6-7—126
6:9—163
12:22—19, 163-64

16:14—55, 164, 165
18:23—29
30:22—187

II Samuel
3:39—187
17:14—164-65

I Kings
2:44—187
11:29—129
22:19—11
22:20ff.—165
22:20-23—56

II Kings
6:12—43

I Chronicles
16:10—71
29:17—71

II Chronicles
10:15—128, 165
22:4—186-87
25:12—158-59
25:16—58
25:17-23—166
29:6—186-87
33:2, 6—186-87
36:5, 9, 12—186-87
36:22—166-67

Ezra
1:1—167

6:22—126, 167
7:6—60
7:13—167, 168
7:13, 16—122
7:15, 16—167, 168
7:27, 28—167-68
10:11—71

Nehemiah
9:6—10, 35
9:35—187

Esther
1:8—71
5:11—29
7:6, 9, 25—187
9:5—71

Job
1—168-69
1:6—11
1:16—169
10:8-9—169
10:9—81
11:11—44
14:4—14
14:5—58, 169-70
15:14—88, 170, 172
19:8-20—170
19:9—29
23:10—170
23:13—170
23:13-14—52, 53
25:4—88, 172
31:4—42, 170-71

33:4-17—171
33:6—81
33:12-13—82
38:4, 12, 31—82
38:4, 31—171
40:2-17, 171
40:4—82
42:2—82, 171-72

Psalm
1:6—68
14—89, 172
14:1-3—191
14:2-3—44
19:1—18
19:12—44
22:30—86
33:6—14
33:6-11—173
33:9—13
33:11—125
36:6—35
40:8—72
50:11—42
51:2—134
51:2, 10—194
51:5—88
51:10—14, 134, 173
56:8—42
65:4—99, 174
89:6—11
89:12—8
90:2—39
102:26-27—39, 174-75
103:20—11

209

103:21—71
104:4—10
104:24—9, 33, 175
104:27—35
104:29—9
104:30—9, 10
105:25—58, 126, 175
115:3—49, 175-76
121:4—38
135:6—49, 176
139—34
139:1-24—176-77
139:2—43
139:2, 15, 16—33
145:9—132
147:4—37
147:5—36
147:10-11—71
148:5—10
149:4—71

Proverbs
3:19—33
5:21—43
8:22—39
11:1, 20—71
12:22—71
14:35—71
15:8—71
15:11—43
16:1—59, 60, 178
16:4—20, 178
16:15—71
19:12—71
20:9—134, 173, 194

21:1—60, 61, 125, 178-79, 201
21:12—187
26:23, 26—187
30:12—134, 194

Ecclesiastes
3:15—42
3:21—9

Song of Solomon
4:16—97

Isaiah
1:16, 17—133, 193
4:5—14
6—11, 181-82
6:1-3—29
8:16-18—137
19:14—182
19:17—60
29:16—80, 182
40:12-17—182-84
40:13—39
40:13-15—74
40:26—16, 37
41:22—41
42:1—63
42:5—11
43:7—20, 184
43:10—63, 184
43:21—184
44:6—19
45—184ff.
45:7—11, 190
45:9—80

210

45:12—188
45:13—188
46:10—38, 50, 68, 125
46:10-11—189
46:13—20
47:7—19
48:12—19
49—190-91
50:4-5—93
52:13—63
53—189ff.
53:1—98
53:10—86
55:11—76, 190
56:2—187
57:1—187
57:15—38
57:19—15
59:7, 15—187
60—191
60:1-2—29
60:19-21—192
60-21—20
61:3—20
64:8—80, 192-93
65:9—192
65:12—187
65:15—192
65:17—15
65:22—192
66—192
66:4—187

Jeremiah
4:4—135, 193

10:12—33
13:13-14—60
17:9—88, 193
18:6—81, 193
23:24—34
32:17—128, 193-94
33:22—37

Lamentations
3:37-38—195-96
3:38—61

Ezekiel
1:28—29
11:19—98, 196, 197, 202
18—201ff.
18:2, 4, 20—202
18:19, 21, 22, 27, 28, 31—202
18:23, 32—202
18:25, 32—201-2
18:31—202-3
21:19—15
23:47—16
33—201, 203
36:25—194
36:25-27—14, 98, 134, 196ff.,
    202
37—88, 198ff., 202
37:4—93
37:15-20—200

Daniel
4:35—51, 203-4
5:27—29
11:36—52, 53, 204

Amos
3:2—68

Haggai
1:8—71

Zechariah
12:10—109, 204

Malachi
4—155

Matthew
1:21—86
3:9—94
5:45—132
6:32—35
10:30—43
11:26—73
12:27—137
22:32—5
23:13—138
23:37—136
26:53-54—61
28:19-20—149

Mark
10:21—138

Luke
2:9—29
2:14—72
10:21—73
19:41—138
22:11—43

22:22—62
22:42—138
24:25—5

John
1:1—37
1:12-13—94, 100
1:13—197
2:24-25—36
3:6—95
3:8—97
5:21—97
5:24-25—91ff.
6:37, 39—86
6:64—37
7:30—64
8:20—64
8:43—91, 93
8:47—93
10:3—87
10:3, 16, 27—93
10:27-28—86
12:38-39—98, 133
13:1—64
15:8—21
15:16—98
17—86
17:1—64
17:1, 4, 5—29
21:17—35-36

Acts
2:1-2—97
2:23—62
4:27-28—63

5:31—108
7:2—137
7:51—139
8:10—103
10—126
10:42—64
11:18—108
11:21—105
13:48—98
15:17-18—47
15:18—38
17:24-28—34, 64, 176
17:24—12
17:26—170
19:44—137
20:26-27—149
22:1—137
22:11—29
26:18—98

Romans
1:7—3
2:10, 14, 25—202
2:29—135, 195
3:10—89
3:20—89, 134, 194
3:23—80, 89
4:17—41
5:12-21—202
6:13—90
8:6—90
8:28-30—66, 74, 78
8:31—69
9—75ff.
9:6—76f.

9:11—79
9:16—82
9:17—30
9:20, 21—81, 118
9:22—83
10:1—72
11—77
11:7-8—84
11:21—118
11:22—132
11:36—18
12:3—105

I Corinthians
1:28—41
2:5—149
2:7—69
2:11—38
4:5—35
6:11—103
10:6—103
11:7—20
12:9—106
15:41—29

II Corinthians
3:7, 18—29
4:4, 6—29, 99
7:10—109

Galatians
1:1—27
2:20—100
3:7—94
6:16—78

213

Ephesians
1:4—70, 78, 79
1:4-11—74
1:5—20, 69, 70
1:5, 9—74
1:11—69, 74, 121
2:1—90, 99
2:3—95
2:5—99
2:8—102ff., 153n.
3:8-10—21ff.
3:9—13
3:9-11—23
6:23—105

Philippians
1:5—72
1:29—105
2:12-13—73, 99, 120

Colossians
1:13-16—13
2:11—135, 195
2:13—90

I Thessalonians
5:9—99

II Thessalonians
1:10—21
1:11—73
2:13-14—100

I Timothy
1:17—54

II Timothy
2:19—87, 117
2:25—108
3:16—5

Hebrews
1:3—29
2:10—18
3:4—13
4:12—43
4:13—35
5:12ff.—148
11:3—13

James
1:18—100

I Peter
2:19—103
4:11—21

II Peter
2:17—103
3:1, 3, 4, 8, 14, 15, 17—141
3:9—140ff.

Jude
12—103

Revelation
1:8—17, 20
4:8—17
4:11—16
11:17—17
13:8—87, 190

214

15:3—17
16:7, 21, 22—17
16:14—17
17:8—190
19:6—17
19:15—17
21:27—87